TIME FOR TRUTH

DOM

and to CJ
with love,
in a time when living free requires
choice as well as courage and clear thinking

CONTENTS

INTRODUCTION

BUT NOT THROUGH ME

The year 1989 was widely described as the 'year of the century'. Set off by the stunning collapse of the Soviet Empire, a tidal wave of euphoria swelled around the world, exaggerated though understandable. Almost everyone who lived through those days has their own vivid memories of the intoxicating events. For some it was the wild dismantling of the Berlin Wall. For others it was the flowers thrusting jauntily out of the gun barrels of Soviet tanks. For still others it was the toppling statues of the discredited man-gods, Marx, Lenin, and Stalin. Joyously and irrepressibly, freedom was breaking out all over the world.

The images most sharply etched in my mind, which a friend witnessed in person, were of the vast rallies in November 1989 at the climax of the 'Velvet Revolution' in Prague. Night after night crowds of more than a quarter of a million packed Wenceslas Square, mesmerized by the stirring addresses of the slim, boyish, moustached figure of then dissident, later President, Václav Havel. Again and again, as the speakers painted the stark contrasts between the revolutionaries and the regime, the quick-witted Czech crowd broke out into a chant:

'We–are–not–like–them! We–are–not–like–them!'

The contrast that first triggered the refrain was the dissidents' refusal to counter violence with violence. Another – a central defining feature of the Czech revolution – was the contrast between truth and lies. 'They', meaning the Soviet regime, 'are people of lies and propaganda.' 'We', the revolutionaries, 'are people of truth.' Or as the motto of the Charter 77 Movement expressed it boldly, 'Truth prevails for those who live in truth.'

For Havel, as a philosopher and a Czech, truth had always been inspiring. One of his heroes, the philosopher Thomas Masaryk, who was the founder and president of the Czechoslovakian Republic (1918–35), had inscribed the motto 'Truth prevails' on the national banner that flies above Prague's castle. A generation later, Jan Patoèka, another philosopher-hero, chose the motto 'Live in truth' when the Charter 77 Movement was founded. Living in truth, Havel realized, was the dissidents' only possible antidote to living a lie. Far deeper than a clash of political power, living in truth sprang from 'the theatre of the spirit and the conscience of society'.

The same claim was staked out by the Soviet Union's own one-man dissident movement, Aleksandr Solzhenitsyn, in his Nobel speech: 'One word of truth outweighs the entire world.' The explosiveness of truth had shown itself even earlier in 1966 when Solzhenitsyn, then little known, gave a public reading at the Soviet Union's Lasarev Institute. That night, instead of just reading from his novels, Solzhenitsyn launched a blistering attack on censorship and the KGB. The effect was electrifying. Almost every sentence, the writer later recalled, 'scorched the air like gunpowder! How those people must have yearned for truth! Oh God, how badly they wanted to hear the truth!'

As Solzhenitsyn and the leaders of the Velvet Revolution saw with a clarity chiselled in courage, there were only two ways to bring down the might of Soviet tyranny. One was to trump Soviet force physically, which was impossible for a tiny handful of dissidents in a day of SS-20 missiles and the KGB. The other was to counter physical force with moral, staking their stand on the conviction that truth would outweigh lies and the whole machinery of propaganda, deception, and terror. They chose the latter, and the unthinkable happened. They won.

Havel had predicted the outcome eleven years before, in 1978, in his essay 'The Power of the Powerless':

> For the crust presented by the life of lies is made of strange stuff. As long as it seals off hermetically the entire society, it appears to be made of stone. But the moment someone breaks through in one place, when one person cries out, 'The emperor is naked!' – when a single person breaks the rules of the game, thus exposing it as a game – everything suddenly appears in another light and the whole crust seems then to be made of a tissue on the point of tearing and disintegrating uncontrollably.

Truth is dead

The years since 1989 have added perspective and background to those stirring revolutionary events, shading and softening the bold outlines to give a richer picture. But today one thing stands out even starker than before. Citizens of the West who rightly rose to applaud the dissidents' courageous stand on truth now belong to a culture that no longer holds a view of truth on which to make such a stand.

One word of truth outweighs the entire world? Truth prevails for those who live in truth? A public hungry to hear the truth? Hardly – or at least, not here and now. 'The truth shall set you free' may be the most popular university motto across the western world, but while the text still adorns the walls, the truth no longer animates the minds.

In both popular and elite circles in the West a very different opinion, loosely called the postmodern move-ment, is becoming dominant. Within it, truth is dead. Truth in any objective or absolute sense, truth that is independent of the mind of the knower, no longer exists. At best, truth is relative – it's all a matter of interpretation and it all depends on the perspective. At worst, truth is 'socially constructed' – merely a matter of human con-vention and a testament to the community that believes it and the power that established it.

A simple way to illustrate this lies in the story of the three cricket umpires debating their different philosophies of umpiring. 'There's no-balls and there's wides,' says the first, 'and *I call them the way they are.*'

'No!' exclaims the second umpire. 'That's arrogant. There's no-balls and there's wides and *I call them the way I see it.*'

'That's no better,' says the third. 'Why beat around the bush? Why not be realistic about what we do? There's no-balls and there's wides and *they're nothing till I call them.*'

The first umpire represents the traditional view of truth

– objective, independent of the mind of the knower, and there to be discovered. The second umpire speaks for moderate relativism – truth 'as each person sees it' according to his or her perspective and interpretation. And the third umpire bluntly expresses the radically relativist, or postmodern, position – 'truth' is not there to be discovered; it is for each of us to create for ourselves.

Thus in a postmodern world, the question is no longer 'Is it true?' but rather '*Whose* truth is it?' and '*Which* power stands to gain?' As Hitler's propaganda minister Joseph Göbbels declared in a foretaste of postmodernism, 'We do not talk to say something but to obtain a certain effect.'

Reality, then, is only a state of mind of the 'enchanted loom' of the brain. 'Truth' is created, not discovered, and to be correct we should say 'truths', not truth. All cultures are equal, each in its own special way. Lying is no longer lying if you are 'telling your own personal truth' or speaking for the 'larger truth' of your group. No judgments can be made, and there can be no 'reform' or 'moral progress', because that implies standards by which to judge the forward movement. As Friedrich Nietzsche wrote typically, 'Truths are illusions about which one has forgotten that this is what they are.' Not surprisingly, what remains in the West is a world of lies, hype, and spin.

So truth is dead and knowledge is only power. Dismantle the high-sounding claims to truth, it is said, and you come face to face with the power-driven agendas of race, class, gender, and generation. To believe otherwise is seen to be naïve, obscurantist, or reactionary. Worse, it is to be morally blind to the dark impulses that poison the traditional distinctions between truth and falsehood, right and wrong, and character and image.

Au contraire

My purpose here is to argue exactly the opposite. For a start, far from ushering in a brave, new world of greater enlightenment and freedom, the radical scepticism of today's new sophists actually sounds the death-knell of western civilization in general, including the momentous American experiment. Postmodernism's current assault on truth is the cultural vanguard of developments that amount to a profound crisis of cultural authority in the West – a crisis in the beliefs, traditions, and ideals that have been decisive for western civilization to this point.

More importantly still, far from being a naïve and reactionary notion, truth is one of the simplest, most precious gifts without which we would not be able to handle reality or negotiate life. Neither unhealthy nor repressive, truth is a vital requirement not only for individuals who would live a good life but for free societies that would remain free.

In short, I will argue that truth is far from dead. It is alive and well and, in an important sense, undeniable. And it is far from inconsequential.

Truth matters supremely because, in the end, without truth there is no freedom. Truth, in fact, is not only essential to freedom; it *is* freedom, and the only way to a free life lies in becoming a person of truth and learning to live in truth. Living in truth is the secret of living free.

Clear expectations

Let me be clear about six other things from the start. First, this is a small book on a big topic and does not pretend to be a comprehensive study of postmodernism or its assault on truth. That would require a longer treatment and a more specialized approach. Although the argument here could be extended in just such a way, that is not my intention, for such an examination would lift the discussion out of the reach of thoughtful people from all walks of life.

As philosopher Bertrand Russell remarked about another philosophical enquiry, all too often 'the technical refinements add very little except controversy & long words'. But truth is no more the monopoly of radical, jargon-wielding modern theorists than of those they view as stuffy, traditionalist philosophers. Truth, because it is our basic human handle on reality, is vital to us all – teenagers as well as teachers, mothers as much as judges, taxi-drivers and school caretakers no less than journalists and university professors.

Second, my primary concern over the crisis of truth is practical, public, and positive, not simply theoretical and analytical. Philosophical issues do lie at the heart of both the roots and the resolution of the crisis, for what is now working out in press conferences, lawcourts, school classrooms, doctors' surgeries, and other forums has flowed from the world of ideas. But few of us are philosophers, and the answer will not come from ideas alone.

As we will see, stirring people to wake up requires more practical and public considerations, just as providing culture-wide solutions requires a more radical and positive approach. Our challenge today is not to lament, protest, or simply talk about the crisis of truth in one of a hundred ways. Rather, it is to do something about it by becoming people of truth and learning to live free.

Third, I am expressly not arguing against the post-modern view of truth on behalf of the modern view. As will become clear, I regard each as bad as the other. The tensions created by each are equally unacceptable and the public damage of each is equally disastrous.

On the one hand, the postmodern position is too cynical and uncertain for a good life and for free societies. It has been called the 'genealogists' view of truth' because it attempts to trace the pedigree of truth and virtue back to its roots in power and bias. But on the other hand, the modern position is naïve and too certain in the wrong way. It, in turn, has been called the 'encyclopaedists' view of truth' because it sees truth as objective and classifiable on the basis of unaided reason alone.

Of the two, the postmodern view is unquestionably the more dangerous today – not because it is postmodern, but because it is current. Postmodernism, in fact, is the mirror image of modernism and is born of its deficiencies. It is therefore equally confused and equally confusing, but in a reverse way.

Clearly, we urgently need a third position – the 'faith community/tradition view of truth' – which the Jewish and Christian faiths represent. This position gives a proper place to the importance of presuppositions in thought, the importance of tradition in handing down thinking, and the necessity of a transcendent reference in human knowledge. It also includes the strengths of the other two views while avoiding the weaknesses of each, but faces its own supreme challenge.

Ever since the Enlightenment, many Jewish and Christian believers have been cut off from the greatness of their own heritages – Jews by the equation that 'secularity equals security', and Christians by the conviction that faith and reason are marching in opposite directions. Whether these communities of faith will remedy these weaknesses and stand together at key points is one of the vital questions at the beginning of the twenty-first century.

Fourth, I will argue that postmodernism as a movement, far from being small and theoretical, represents a watershed moment particularly for the United States in its global dominance. Many of the world's challenges at the start of the new millennium stem from the strains and tensions of transition – South Africa, for example, represents countries undergoing the transition from colonialism to post-colonialism, just as Russia represents countries undergoing the transition from communism to post-communism. But both of these pale beside the transition now taking place in America as it moves from modernism to postmodernism, with repercussions for all of the West.

Important because currently the world's 'lead society', the United States is the child of the Protestant Reformation and the Enlightenment. America has always been a nation by intention and by ideas – a key aspect of its being the *novus ordo saeculorum* (new order of the ages). Yet postmodernism emphatically repudiates both sides of this heritage, the Christian and the modern, and creates a profound crisis of cultural authority in the beliefs, both civic and religious, that have made America what it is. Not only does the day-to-day life of its citizens change as a consequence; the very meaning of the American experiment is altered beyond recognition and beyond renewal, and with it the dominant way of understanding and perpetuating western civilization.

Fifth, I will argue that the issue of truth has a far deeper moral and political seriousness than it receives now. In each generation the price of lying is pegged to the price of truth, which means that both are held cheaply today. I am not arguing the absolutist position that lying is always wrong, for in a world like ours it is sometimes essential. There are numerous 'morally permissible lies': in the opening chapters of Exodus, for example, the Hebrew midwives lie to Pharaoh to save their baby boys from death. As Winston Churchill said after the Teheran Conference in 1943 about Allied secrecy over plans to invade Europe, 'Truth is so precious that she must often be attended by a bodyguard of lies.'

But it is another thing altogether to void the difference between truth and lying. And it is another thing still to see lying only as a minor problem, a 'utility sin' in the sense that boasting is lying in the service of pride, slander is lying in the service of envy, and so on. The latter point may be true as far as it goes, but it is not the whole story. And it becomes pernicious when people go on from there to trivialize lying as a form of social and semantic gamesmanship of no consequence.

'You shall not bear false witness,' the ninth commandment thundered from Sinai. From beginning to end, the Bible declares that God detests lying and that deception is a major root of evil in our world. Defined as 'an attempt to deceive without the other's consent', a lie is a fundamental breach of the human contract to speak the truth. Thus to treat lying, falsehood, evasiveness, mendacity, and carelessness with words as only minor problems – whimsies with words – hands a dangerous alibi to the powerful and creates a postmodern sanctuary that the unscrupulous have already exploited (witness the Clinton/Lewinsky scandal) and are certain to take advantage of even further. As Walter Lippmann wrote, 'There can be no liberty for a community that lacks the means by which to detect lies.'

Lastly, in writing about living in truth and being people of truth, I am not in any way claiming to live up to the vision without fail. In fact, much of what is written here comes from insights born of not doing so.

The discipline of living in truth is urgent today because modern life reduces community and accountability to its thinnest, thereby tempting us to live in a shadow world of anonymity and non-responsibility where all cats are grey. In such a world, becoming people of truth is the deepest secret of integrity and the highest form of taking responsibility for ourselves and our own lives.

Two by two

Our approach here will be to examine the postmodern crisis of truth through a series of pairs. In chapters 1 and 2 we explore the impact of the crisis of truth on two companion crises: the crisis of ethics and the crisis of character. In chapter 3, we look at the unavoidable example of postmodernism's influence on America at two levels, the global and national, and what the outcome means for western civilization. In chapter 4 we examine two arguments for the importance of truth in a day when many people don't seem to care. In chapter 5 we discuss two strategies for responding to those who insist on rejecting truth, and in chapter 6 we look at two tough choices with which the discipline of living in truth always confronts us.

As we will see by the end of the argument, an understanding of truth and the present crisis of truth opens up many challenges and options to us along the way. But they are not all relative. Nor are they inconsequential. If truth is truth, then differences make a difference – not just between truth and lies, but between intimacy and alienation in relationships, between harmony and conflict in neighbourhoods, between efficiency and incompetence in business, between reliability and fraud in science and journalism, between trust and suspicion in leadership, between freedom and tyranny in government, and even between life and death. Certainly, the choices are ours, but so also are the consequences.

And when it comes to truth, the outcome affects not only individuals but nations and even civilizations. What starts looking like a small and abstract issue ends with titanic, public consequences for all who love freedom and justice. 'I cannot overcome the impression', Havel wrote, 'that Western culture is threatened far more by itself than by SS-20 rockets.' But as he warned, and as we will see throughout, the deepest challenge is not to talk about truth but to live in truth. As Albert Camus wrote in his journal, 'truth cannot be achieved without a true life'.

This is no time for grandiosity or illusions. Living free is far from easy. Our living in truth will not automatically mean the disappearance of living in the lie. We have no guarantee of a Solzhenitsyn-like shout that starts an avalanche in the mountains. For the lies of western society – particularly as they are compounded by the 'culture cartel' of postmodern academia, advertising, entertainment, and youth culture – are more seductive and enduring than those of communist society.

Be that as it may. If we live in truth and become people of truth, our primary responsibility will be evident: ourselves. Our overarching life-task will be clear: to seek the truth, speak the truth, and live the truth. And the one effective stand that no-one can take from us will be certain: as Solzhenitsyn declared in his Nobel address, 'Let the lie come into the world, even dominate the world, but not through me.'

ONE

BACK TO THE MORAL STONE AGE

It was a warm California night, but the lecturer felt 'shivery, chilled to the bone'. The outrageous had outraged no-one. The unthinkable was being thought all too thoughtlessly. After all her years as a veteran of California adult-education, she had heard what she never expected to hear. Her response was profound dismay: 'No-one in the whole class of twenty ostensibly intelligent individuals would go out on a limb and take a stand against human sacrifice.'

The short story under discussion was Shirley Jackson's 'The Lottery'. Set in a small town somewhere in rural America, the townsfolk are gathering for some ritual obviously critical for the well-being of the crops and the community. At the centre of everyone's thoughts is a lottery. The build-up to the draw gathers momentum from Jackson's skilful weaving of the down-to-earth realism of the story with the mounting suspense of the unnamed event about to unfold.

Suddenly, in a stunning denouement, everything becomes grotesquely clear. The draw is for a human sacrifice. Tessie Hutchinson, wife, mother, and neighbour, chooses the slip of paper with the black spot. Instantly she finds herself isolated in the centre of a cleared space. Even her son, little Davy, has pebbles in his hand.

'Come on, come on, everyone,' Old Man Warner urges the villagers – and they do.

'It isn't fair, it isn't right,' Mrs Hutchinson screams, but there is no stopping the ritual. The story ends with a sickening thud: 'and then they were upon her'.

When the *New Yorker* first published 'The Lottery' in 1948, it was deluged by letters in a storm of outrage. In the robustly moral climate of victorious, post-war America, the very idea of conformity to such a ritual was outrageous. Human sacrifice was unthinkable; it simply couldn't happen in America. Late-1940s America may have been far too conformist for the later 1960s generation, but the story's moral – the dangers of 'going along' in blind social conformity – found a passionate response in the generation that had stood up to Hitler.

But times change. Since the publication of the story, countless secondary-school classes have read and discussed it, and the reactions it triggers have changed along with the students. In fact, student responses give a remarkably accurate seismograph reading of the wider shifts in society over the years.

It was these changes that Kay Haugaard, lecturer in southern California, had noted in her students from more than two decades of teaching creative writing. Starting in 1970, she observed that her first students, ranging from eighteen-year-olds to eighty-year-olds, were still 'shocked into giggles or frowns at the sound of naughty words' in either the published stories or students' work.

Slowly the writing and the responses changed. The shift started with the increased violence of the stories of Vietnam veterans that talked of killing, maiming, brutal deaths, and bizarre sexual encounters with Vietnamese prostitutes. Then, successively, it was the turn of homosexual narratives, lesbian testimonies, and varied writings on civil rights, sexual liberation, and multiculturalism. Gradually the explicitness of the anger, victimhood, and lewdness led to a noticeable coarsening of the writing and a jadedness of the responses.

Yet, during all those years, 'The Lottery' was one story that had always managed to elicit a strong moral response. The tale was so well told, the moral so powerful, and the ritual so shocking, that at least this story could engage the students' sense of right and wrong.

Until the 1990s, that is. One night Haugaard encountered a class that registered no moral response at all.

'The end was neat!' one woman said.

'It was all right. It wasn't that great,' another repeated.

'They just do it,' yet another argued, 'It's their ritual.'

Haugaard's concern mounted dramatically as the unconcern deepened in the room. 'I was stunned,' she later wrote after questioning Beth, a stylish student in her forties, that 'this was the woman who wrote so passionately about saving the whales, of concern for the rain forests, of her rescue and tender care for a stray dog.'

But more was to come. Another student, Richard, put forward a psychological theory espousing the social value of a certain amount of bloodshed. 'It almost seems a need,' he concluded in cool, reasonable tones.

Finally, after Haugaard had broken her normal custom and expressed her own moral position forcefully, a nurse in her fifties summed up the discussion: 'Well, I teach a course for our hospital personnel in multicultural understanding, and if it's a part of a person's culture, we are taught not to judge, and if it has worked for them ...'

'At this point I gave up,' Haugaard reported in *The Chronicle of Higher Education*. 'No-one in the whole class of more than twenty ostensibly intelligent individuals would go out on a limb and take a stand against human sacrifice.'

Thou shalt not judge

Kay Haugaard's account is profoundly disturbing for both moral and political reasons, but it is hardly surprising. In large parts of the West, the crisis of truth has spawned two other companion crises: one in ethics, which we will examine in this chapter, and another in character, which we will look at in the next. The sources of these crises lie in intellectual and social roots respectively.

As the reaction to 'The Lottery' reveals, the late-1960s slogan painted on the wall at the Sorbonne, 'It is forbidden to forbid' now covers thoughts and analysis as well as actions. Censuring is commonly confused with censoring, and moral judgment has been paralysed. Many discussions are now void of a backstop crime or evil that will elicit universal condemnation. Even the Holocaust is increasingly 'personally deplored' but not morally condemned.

Earlier, playwright Bertold Brecht claimed that the eleventh commandment of the modern world was 'Be good to yourself.' Today it has been replaced by a new candidate: 'Thou shalt not judge.' In such a world, what follows is simple. When nothing can be judged except judgment itself – 'judgmentalism' – the barriers between the unthinkable, acceptable, and do-able collapse entirely. And then, since life goes on and the sky doesn't fall, people draw the conclusion that the original concern was unfounded. Lighten up, the newly amoral say as they skip forward blithely, complicit in their own corruption.

But what *is* surprising, perhaps, is that the contemporary crisis of truth, ethics, and character is playing out in the midst of an extraordinary resurgence of interest in ethics around the western world. For instance, a survey by the Hastings Center claims that the United States alone now offers over 11,000 courses in applied ethics that tackle all manner of ethical problems in business, politics, medicine, science, engineering, and social work. These courses are backed by thousands of experts through hundreds of textbooks, dozens of journals, and some staggeringly generous financial grants.

Some people interpret this explosion of interest in ethics as the return to a morally robust era. Right up to the end of the nineteenth century, the most important course in an American student's college career was moral philosophy, or what we today call ethics. The course was seen as the crowning unit in the senior year, usually taught by the college president himself. As President James Monroe said of such classes, 'The question to be asked at the end of an educational step is not "What has the student learned?" but "What has the student become?"'

At a different level, both MTV and the *New York Times* in the nineties took up the topic of the seven deadly sins. Surely, it is said, we are witnessing the beginning of an ethical revival.

Beneath the surface

Ours an age of deepened morality? Far from it. In fact, this renewed enthusiasm for ethics is hardly cause for celebration. For one thing, morality is like health:

preoccupation with it is often a sign of illness, not vitality. For another thing, a closer look at the resurgence is not so reassuring.

First, part of the renewed interest is simply fashionable and transient. As one commentator put it, 'In our low-fat, low-conscience culture, SinLite has found shelf space alongside other low-guilt pleasures.' Or in the words of MTV, 'A little lust, pride, sloth, and gluttony – in moderation – are fun, and that's what keeps your heart beating.'

Second, much of today's focus is on 'prevention ethics' rather than on principled ethics. It is more concerned with 'not being caught' (or sued or exposed in the press) than with doing right. Besides, what Oscar Wilde said cynically a century ago is uncomfortably apt in the climate of today's culture wars: 'Morality is simply the attitude we adopt toward people we personally dislike.'

Third, even where good ethics is taught in a good way, it is usually more social in nature than personal. That is, what matters for the politically correct is to hold the right views, not to practise them. What is seen as important are issues related to corporations, schools, courts, governments, and the treatment of the environment – not the individual's virtue and responsibility that underlie these secondary issues.

As ethicist Christina Sommers writes, 'A glance at a typical anthology of a college course in ethics reveals that most of what the student will read is directed toward analyzing and criticizing policies on such issues as punishment, recombinant DNA research, abortion, and euthanasia … Inevitably the student gets the idea that applying ethics to modern life is mainly a matter of being for or against some social policy.'

Fourth, and worse still, the current ethics is often taught with a shallow view of human nature and an even more superficial view of evil in human society. For example, such topics as hypocrisy, self-deception, self-ishness, and cruelty rarely come up. And the place of envy in politics, greed in the economy, lust in the fashion industry, and violence in the entertainment business is rarely probed.

Fifth, and worst of all, the present preoccupation with ethics in elite intellectual centres has an element of absurdity because they have no moral content left to teach. The fruit of the western universities in the last two hundred years has been to destroy the possibility of any moral knowledge on which to pursue moral formation.

Derek Bok, President of Harvard University, expressed this point guardedly: 'Today's course in applied ethics does not seek to convey a set of moral truths, but tries to encourage the student to think carefully about complex moral issues ... The principal aim of the course is not to impart "right answers" but to make the student more perceptive in detecting ethical problems when they arise.'

Philosopher Dallas Willard was more blunt. Had President Bok 'strolled across Harvard Yard to Emerson Hall and consulted with some of the most influential thinkers in our nation, he would have discovered that there now is no recognized moral knowledge upon which projects of fostering moral development could be based. There is now not a single moral conclusion about behavior or character traits that a teacher could base a student's grade on – not even those most dear to educators, concerning fairness and diversity.'

With no moral conclusions left, all that remains is ever more clever talk about ethics – and even that is complicated and controversial. As Bertrand Russell observed well back in the last century: 'Where ethics is concerned, I hold that, so far as fundamentals are concerned, it is impossible to produce conclusive intellectual arguments ... In a fundamental question of ethics I do not think a theoretical argument is possible.'

This result is shocking for a civilization that once took pride in progress and moral reform – reform by an accepted moral standard by which such evils as persecution and chattel slavery were pronounced unacceptable and wrong. Technologically, western civilization has advanced to the age of space and cyberspace, but ethically we have regressed. 'We have been thrown back', Christina Sommers writes, 'into a moral Stone Age; many young people are totally unaffected by thousands of years of moral experience and moral progress.'

'Grey is the color of truth,' George McBundy wrote in defence of the Vietnam War. Only a few decades later the grey has deepened to near-black. Today many people feel that trying to navigate the moral confusion of modern society is like driving through London or New York without a map and with all the traffic lights turned off.

Defining deviancy down

What lies behind this widespread moral confusion? One factor is simple: a lack of serious analysis of why we have an ethics crisis in the first place, which, in turn, reinforces the obvious shortcomings in the so-called revival of ethics. Most attention is directed at symptoms, not causes; few people dig down to the roots.

For example, few Americans understand that their country, because of the convictions of its founders, has a realistic view of evil embedded in its constitutional checks and balances. Yet US psychologist Karl Menninger's 1973 book, *Whatever Became of Sin?*, was not only a startling title but a sobering benchmark for them to gauge the slippage from their founders' position. The notion of evil, Menninger argued, had slid from being 'sin' defined theologically, to being 'crime' defined legally, to being 'sickness' defined only in psychological categories. In US Senator Daniel Patrick Moynihan's more recent analysis, Americans have 'defined deviancy down'. What was 'deviant' fifty years ago in America is today just par for the course.

The wider moral confusion in the West (for similar problems exist in other modern countries) can be probed best with the help of three terms: 'permissive', 'transgressive', and 'remissive'. Fyodor Dostoyevsky captured the first a hundred years ago in his famous refrain in *The Brothers Karamazov*: if God is dead, and there is no future life, 'nothing would be immoral any longer, everything would be permitted'.

The developments of a century later show that the consequences are not limited to morals. If 'God is dead', all sorts of other things die too, including truth, selfhood, character, the power of words to describe reality and for some people even reality itself. For the sceptic who pushes, there is no stopping point, at least in thought.

The second term, *transgressive*, found its classic expression in the 1968 Sorbonne slogan mentioned earlier, 'It is forbidden to forbid.' This was later popularized by basketball player Denis Rodmann as 'Bad as I wanna be', and exemplified by the choreographer of rock star Madonna: 'Madonna told me to break every rule I could think of, and then when I was done to make up some new ones and break them.'

Of course, there are limits to transgressing, which under postmodern conditions becomes the exhibitionism of transgressing: chaos for society and boredom for the transgressor. For instance, shock-rocker Marilyn Manson recently complained, 'We can't go any further without starting over ... What other violence can you show? What other drug can you do? What other thing can you get pierced? It's all been done.' But even short of this point, the costs of the moral vandalism are enormous, not least because the transgressors wreak their havoc in the name of specious freedom that others desire to copy.

The third term, *remissive*, comes up repeatedly when people try to describe the moral crisis and grope for terms that capture its overwhelming and snowballing nature. Society they say, is 'eroding', 'unravelling', 'fraying', 'melting down', and the like. Or, as one political leader expressed it during the scandals swirling around the Clinton presidency: 'You can stop a flood by putting your finger in the dike, but how do you stop a mudslide?'

Shots from the old artilleryman

The most powerful philosophical source of the crisis of truth is the writings of Friedrich Nietzsche in the 1880s. Weak, sickly, physically shortsighted, racked by tremendous pain, little known and less read, Nietzsche in those years shuttled between Torino in Italy, Ezes-sur-Nice in France, and Sils Maria, near the modern ski resort of St Moritz, in Switzerland. In the few hours of the days he was able to write, he poured out a series of books so revolutionary that the twentieth century has been described as a footnote on his thought.

The self-proclaimed 'immoralist', 'anti-Christ', and 'conqueror of God', Nietzsche ranked his *Zarathustra* as 'a fifth Gospel' and styled himself the 'teacher of mistrust of truth'. He also called himself the 'old artilleryman' because of brief service in the Franco-Prussian War, and described his way of analysis as doing philosophy 'with a hammer'.

Clearly, he never suffered from false modesty. 'I know my fate,' he wrote in *Ecce Homo*. 'One day my name will be associated with the memory of … a crisis without equal on earth, the most profound collision of conscience, a decision that was conjured up *against* everything that had been believed, demanded, hallowed so far. I am no man. I am dynamite.'

More prosaically, Nietzsche mounted a furious assault on the traditional view of truth and ethics from two sides. From one better-known side he relativized truth through his notion of 'perspectivism': 'There are many kinds of eyes, and consequently there are many kinds of "truths", and consequently there is no truth.'

And from the other less-known side he rationalized truth through his notion of the 'genealogy of morals'. He claimed that truth and virtue, if their family trees were traced back, were far from self-evident, straightforward, and noble, but were rooted in resentments and ignoble vices. Thus 'truth', he said, was a mask for the will to power; 'pity' was the poison of resentment; and 'virtue' a pious form of hypocrisy whereby the 'slave class' gained its revenge on the 'master class', the 'herd' on the 'hero'. In short, 'faith' is servile, snivelling, and insincere, a sanctimonious mask to cover a can of emotional worms.

In Nietzsche's final writings, especially *The Will to Power*, power was central to everything. 'This world is the will to power – and nothing besides! And you yourselves are also this will to power – and nothing besides!' To feel their intoxication, his late writings need to be read when alone, unhurried, and preferably in a majestic setting like the Alps or the Rockies. Little wonder so many have read Nietzsche and been drawn to their destruction like moths to a flame. What extreme sports are to today's thrill-seekers, Nietzsche is to the rare mind and spirit: the extreme philosopher whose most audacious thoughts were written at the very rim of his own sanity before he plunged over.

After all, Nietzsche writes in *Beyond Good and Evil*, the higher truths are only for heroes and are considerably dangerous: 'Indeed, it may be a characteristic of existence that those who would know it completely would perish, in which case the strength of a spirit should be measured according to how much of the 'truth' one could still barely endure – or to put it more clearly, to what degree one would *require* it to be thinned down, shrouded, sweetened, falsified.'

Traditionally, power without wisdom and virtue has been viewed as dangerous. In *The Wild Ass's Skin*, Honoré de Balzac observed that possessing power does not mean knowing how to use it. 'A sceptre is a toy for a child, an axe for a Richelieu, and for Napoleon a lever with which to move the earth. Power leaves our natures untouched and confers greatness only on the great.' Sir Winston Churchill wrote similarly, reflecting on the Second World War, 'Power, for the sake of lording it over fellow creatures or adding to personal pomp, is rightly judged base.'

In stark contrast, today's postmodernists who follow Nietzsche view power as everything. From philosophy to literary theory to evolutionary psychology to legal studies to lawcourts to the airwaves and election campaigns, everything is power. All else is flummery and illusion.

Later, in chapter 4, we will set out the strategies for responding to these assaults. Here it is important only to underscore how deadly Nietzsche's attacks have proved. Far from assailing one truth-claim or one virtue in the name of another (which has the effect of reinforcing the importance of truth and virtue themselves), he undermines the very notions.

Not only the possibility but the worthwhileness of truth and virtue is emptied of meaning. Whatever someone may profess, things are always other than they pretend, darker and murkier than they make out. Our proper response, we are taught, should be to view every claim with a sense of irony, interpret everything with suspicion, and pursue 'truth' and 'virtue' with the central agenda of unmasking and dismantling them.

Passing through the fiery brook

Nietzsche's philosophical assault on truth and ethics is deadly enough, but it has been joined by an equally lethal assault from the social sciences. Many claim that the discipline of the sociology of knowledge (my own discipline) demonstrates that all human knowledge is not only relative but 'socially constructed', *and nothing more*. That is, what we know is so shaped by our social context that any claim to be true or false, right or wrong, is patently absurd. 'Truth' is only a matter of human convention or social construction.

It is important to say that the best proponents of the sociology of knowledge do not see the discipline as ruling out the importance or possibility of truth. But as popularly understood – in other words, as misunderstood – that is the effect. The reason is obvious. The history of ideas proceeds by tracing a line from thinkers to thoughts to their impact on the world: 'Ideas have consequences.' By contrast, the sociology of knowledge does the opposite, tracing the line from social context to thoughts to thinkers: 'Culture shapes ideas.'

A simple example is the modern attitude toward time. Asians used to say that westerners are 'people with gods on their wrists', while Africans observed that 'all westerners have watches; no westerners have time'. Many modern expressions, such as 'time is money', 'buying time', 'quality time', and 'opportunity costs', attest to this same decisive and almost inescapable sense of modern time – simultaneously pressured and precious.

Yet this modern view of time cannot be traced to any single thinker or school of thought. Rather, our so-called 'clock culture' is just that, the fruit of our modern world of clocks and watches, especially as synchronized with the whole of life in the Industrial Revolution and most especially as accelerated by the 'instant, total capacity' of modern information technology. In this sense our modern view of time is 'socially constructed'.

But does the sociology of knowledge claim that all knowledge is 'socially constructed' *and nothing more* – in other words, not true? Emphatically not. The best sociologists of knowledge (supremely Peter L. Berger) do not presume to make this judgment. Instead, they bracket the question of truth as being outside the jurisdiction of sociology and pass it on to philosophy. They point out that for sociology to judge its own truthfulness would be self-defeating: as Berger says, 'It would be like trying to push a bus on which one was riding.'

The sociology of knowledge, then, should not presume to make a judgment on the *truth* of beliefs. Rather, its province is to analyse the social context of whatever *passes* for knowledge and leave the question of truthfulness to others. There are more tools in the tool box of understanding than this one.

Such modesty and clear thinking, however, have not characterized those (usually not sociologists of knowledge) who brandish the term 'socially constructed' and apply it to everything. In their careless hands the term is used falsely to proclaim that *nothing is true; everything is only socially constructed.* For instance, Blaise Pascal's brilliant observation on how truth is different on different sides of the Pyrenees becomes a blunt, bulldozing attack on all truth and even on what is meant by the Pyrenees.

Not surprisingly, when the sociology of knowledge is misunderstood and misapplied, it compounds the relativism of what is already, in Berger's description, 'an intrinsically debunking discipline' that 'raises the vertigo of relativity to its most furious pitch'. Punning on the name of Ludwig Feuerbach (the debunking philosopher), Berger calls it the 'fiery brook' through which thinking today must pass.

This dramatic language is well justified, but scepticism won't always be wielded with the intensity of a Nietzschean 'Superman'. A generation that sooner or later 'dumbs down' everything to bumper stickers and Hallmark cards can be counted on for user-friendly versions of Nietzscheanism. A current California bumper sticker translates Nietzsche for the Sunshine State: 'There is no right or wrong – only fun or boring.'

Christina Sommers tells of an undergraduate at a US college who remarked innocently after hearing that all knowledge is socially constructed: 'Although the Holocaust may not have happened, it's a perfectly reasonable conceptual hallucination.'

Using Nietzsche's terms, our danger comes not just from the 'supermen' but from the 'last men'. Losing touch with transcendence, secular people would lose a reference point with which to judge themselves and would end up confusing health with happiness and vice versa. 'One has one's little pleasure for the day and one's little pleasure for the night,' Nietzsche commented in *Thus Spake Zarathustra*. 'But one has a regard for health. "We have invented happiness," say the last men, and they blink.'

TWO

WE'RE ALL
SPINMEISTERS NOW

The little town of Chajul in the western highlands of Guatemala is insignificant by world standards. All that it shares with the capital of any nation is its annual enactment of an event in Jerusalem two thousand years ago. Every Lent thousands of pilgrims flock to Chajul, some from as far away as Mexico and El Salvador, to express their devotion. Following a hallowed procession to the whitewashed Catholic church, they carry a larger-than-life statue of Jesus, who implores heaven and staggers under the weight of his cross.

One day in the autumn of 1979 another anguished crowd gathered in the town square of Chajul imploring heaven. They had been summoned to an execution. Arrested by the army, a group of twenty-three local guerrillas had been tortured and were now to be punished publicly. The populace was ordered to witness the spectacle. Among the victims was a sixteen-year-old boy, Petrocinio Menchú, whose family, alerted to his plight, hurried 16 miles overnight to be present at his ordeal.

Soldiers dragged Petrocinio and the other prisoners off the army truck. Commanded to hold themselves in a straight line, most could barely stand at all. Their tortures over several weeks had been brutal, leaving them bloated like bladders. Petrocinio had no fingernails left. The soles of his feet had been beaten to pulp. His wounds were oozing with infection.

Methodically, soldiers took scissors and cut off the prisoners' clothes. They then callously explained how each wound had been inflicted on the tortured bodies. Finally, the commanding officer ordered his men to soak the prisoners in petrol and set them on fire. The victims died hideously, writhing on the ground, the crowd watching horrified and enraged but helpless.

This gruesome description comes at the climax of the book by Petrocinio's twenty-three-year-old sister, *I, Rigoberta Menchú*, published in 1983. It was reprinted endlessly in magazines and recounted dramatically in conferences, the room darkened except for a single spotlight on the young woman who gave her *testimonio* as witness to the massacre. Based on eighteen-and-a-half hours of taped interviews given by Rigoberta Menchú to anthropologist Elizabeth Burgos in Paris, the book propelled the Mayan to international fame and acclaim, including fourteen honorary doctorates, welcoming receptions from Pope John Paul II and many heads of state, awards such as France's Légion d'Honeur, and the climax of it all, the Nobel Prize for peace in 1992.

With all the modern techniques for fabricating famousness that singer Joni Mitchell dubbed the 'star-maker machinery', Menchú's ascent to secular canonization was swift. Almost overnight, she became a celebrity, saint, revolutionary symbol, and world icon.

Left-wing movements were flagging worldwide in 1992, following the collapse of the Soviet Union and the discrediting of communism. But here was a poster girl who simultaneously fulfilled the dreams of the left-wing solidarity movements, the human-rights community, and the movement of ethnic and women's studies in western universities known as multiculturalism. Who better to celebrate the 500th anniversary of Columbus's discovery of America and Europe's domination of native people everywhere than an uneducated but heroic Native American woman?

There was only one problem. A small boy in the form of a dogged anthropology professor at Middlebury College, Vermont, in the United States, blurted out that the empress had no clothes. Closer investigation, confirmed by the *New York Times*, showed that Menchú's book should more appropriately have been awarded the Nobel Prize for literature rather than for peace. Not only did it openly advocate revolutionary violence, which was odd for the peace prize, but it contained huge factual discrepancies and political distortions. And the claim to eyewitness accounts, including the above story, was bogus. Menchú's brother (and parents) had certainly been killed by the army, but not in that way and not in front of her. No-one had been burned alive in the plaza in Chajul.

In the name of 'truth'

Professor David Stoll recounts his reluctant exposé in *Rigoberta Menchú and the Story of All Poor Guatemalans*. The details of the fiction do not concern us here, but Stoll is right to underscore that Menchú's story has important lessons for western attitudes to knowledge and truth.

Predictably, Stoll's charges created a firestorm of

outrage. They were a sacrilege; he was beyond the pale. Explanations and excuses for Menchú were showered down on him. All memories are selective, especially those of victims of trauma. All testimonies are both tailored and exaggerated. It's absurd to hold illiterate people to western standards of journalistic accuracy. And anyway, wasn't Menchú speaking for her 'larger truth' – for all the Guatemalan people, not just herself? Do we reject Martin Luther King Jr just because he plagiarized part of his PhD thesis?

A Spanish lecturer at Wellesley College defended Menchú: 'Whether her book is true or not, I don't care. We should teach our students about the brutality of the Guatemalan military and the US financing of it.' Menchú herself dismissed Stoll's obsession with facts as racism. 'Whites have been writing our history for over five hundred years, and no white anthropologist is going to tell me what I experienced in my own flesh.' As she told the *Washington Post*, 'My truth is that my brother was burned alive.'

To be sure, the issues raised by this story require careful thinking, and the primary consequences reach far outside the West. But the successful campaign for the award of the Nobel Prize and its political exploitation in the West brings the issue squarely back to the western crisis of truth. For as the incident shows, the crisis of truth is not theoretical only. It quickly becomes practical and political because it flows directly into 'political correctness', and thus into 'identity politics' and the manipulation of 'victimhood'.

Naturally no-one likes to be charged with racism, colonialism, or chauvinism. Nor does anyone want to be caught 'blaming the victim' or found 'misrepresenting the voices of the voiceless' with standards and categories 'imposed by outside cultures of domination'. But the upshot is a chilling of journalistic and academic enquiry. Tough questions go unasked, serious investigations remain unpursued, spurious claims stay unchallenged, competing victims' stories are not assessed, and the aggrieved are issued a licence to lie for their 'larger truth'.

The net result is that an icon becomes unassailable. Another emperor or empress parades naked before fawning courtiers. For heaven's sake, don't let anybody admit the possibility that westerners choose 'select victims' in order to meet their own cultural needs. God forbid the thought that in reducing truth to propaganda, we no longer have the means to distinguish between them. A legend is a legend. Let all tongues be silent and all thinking cease. If the legend is our legend too, who cares whether or not it is true?

Needless to say, Menchú's book is not all fiction and her voice is one to listen to and weigh. There are good reasons why *I, Rigoberta Menchú* has been widely welcomed into the canon of university reading lists. But the way it got there, the significance of the claims it makes, and the political use to which it has been put, provide a cautionary tale about the standing of truth in the West today.

Ironically, two of those on the shortlist whom Menchú beat in winning the Nobel Prize in 1992 were Václav Havel and Nelson Mandela. Somehow, the tough-minded approach to truth of Havel's dissident movement and of Mandela's truth commission were not uppermost in the minds of the Oslo jury.

No there there

The creative reinvention of Rigoberta Menchú and her elevation as a political icon is neither new nor unique. A rash of such fictions has broken out recently and much has been written of the more egregious examples: Tawana Brawley's fabrication of rape charges; columnist Mike Barnicle's concocted stories in the *Boston Globe*; NBC television's staged report on the exploding General Motors trucks, later acknowledged to be planted detonations; Mike Davis's *City of Quartz*, an acclaimed academic analysis of Los Angeles now seen to be fraudulent scholarship; Edmund Morris's *Dutch*, his official biography of Ronald Reagan with his fictional self as Reagan's contemporary; and supremely, Norma McCorvey's (a.k.a. Jane Roe) fabricated story of rape, encouraged by pro-abortion leaders, that was so instrumental in the US Supreme Court's 1973 decision, *Roe v. Wade*.

Whether the licence to lie is explicit or implicit, all of these examples pivot on the same sort of truth-twisting in the cause of the Larger Truth that film-maker Oliver Stone used in defending the facts in one of his films: 'Even if I am totally wrong … I am still right … I am essentially right because I am depicting the Evil with a capital E.'

Clearly, reinventions of all sorts are now widely used, and worse still, accepted and approved, in many spheres of western life. Nor should anyone conclude from these examples that such 'creative storytelling' is a monopoly of the Left. The range is inclusive: men, women, liberals, conservatives, serious writers, humorists, leaders, and ordinary people.

What matters is to see where this creative reinvention comes from and to assess its consequences. In the case of the crisis of character, the principal causes are social, not intellectual, and can be illustrated by a very American example, one that is unquestionably trivial, non-political, and non-intellectual. Though the example is American, the scenario has affinities across the western media.

In his autobiography, *Leading with My Chin*, comedian Jay Leno recounts numerous stories of his rise as a young Boston comedian to his hosting the *Tonight Show* as successor to the legendary Johnny Carson. One chapter tells of his appearance on the Dinah Shore talk show where he learned the importance of what in showbiz parlance is called the 'outcue'.

'OK,' said the talent co-ordinator. 'What's your last joke, so the band knows when to play you off?'

'Listen, do I have to give you my last line?' Leno asked. Like all comedians, he hated to have any band step on a laugh and cut off the applause. But eventually he agreed. 'How about if I just say, "*Thank you, thank you very much!*" Twice, OK? And that'll be the cue.'

Unfortunately, Dinah Shore's welcome was so warm and the audience's ovation for his one-line entry was so overwhelming that Leno was taken aback. Flustered, he muttered, 'Thank you, thank you very much.' The band leader looked up in panic, stubbed out his cigarette, brought the band crashing in, and ushered Leno out. Whereupon Dinah Shore smiled even more broadly, the audience went wild with applause, and the interview was over before it started. 'It was the most ridiculous slot of my career,' Leno said ruefully.

An amusing, somewhat embarrassing anecdote in a book full of stories and jokes, Leno's account has only one problem: it didn't happen – or rather it didn't happen to Leno. As a New York journalist brought to light, the incident actually happened to a fellow-comedian and friend of Leno's. But Leno was so delighted by the story that he paid his friend $1,000 for the rights to use the story as his own material for a chapter in his autobiography.

Wags immediately made fun at the comedian's expense. Think of the commercial potential of creating exciting past lives for unexciting public figures. And why not? On modern assumptions, truth cramps one's style; it limits one's possibilities. But when there is no objective truth, there is no core of personhood or character either. 'There is no there there,' as Gertrude Stein said of the city of Oakland. The sky becomes the limit and the possibilities for reinvention are endless.

As Mark Twain, himself a successful reinvention out of the person of Samuel Clemens, said famously, 'The secret of success is sincerity. If you can fake that, you've got it made.' Or as Groucho Marx quipped in the same vein, 'These are my principles, and if you don't like them … well, I have others.' Or as the hip-hop hype of a contemporary advertiser glibly promises the autonomous self of the sneaker consumer: 'Buy our shoe and "U-B-U".'

Alias Mark Twain

Many individuals have displayed a marked talent for 'reinventions and reincarnations'. T. E. Lawrence, for example, was dubbed 'Protean man' and Bob Dylan 'plastic man'. But the ultimate self-invented man was Samuel Langhorne Clemens, who became Mark Twain. At first sight the process appears all fun: 'No man is straitly honest to any but himself and God,' Clemens remarked, and, since he didn't believe in God, he was free to invent creatively. Much of his work is therefore full of attitudes to truth that are comic, casual, and cynical. He played with truth at will.

'Truth is the most valuable thing we have. Let us economize it,' he wrote in 'Pudd'nhead Wilson's New Calendar' for 1897. Or in the same calendar: 'The principal difference between a cat and a lie is that a cat has only nine lives.' As he told George Bernard Shaw, 'Telling the truth's the funniest joke in the world.' Or as he wrote more cynically to a friend, 'I like the truth sometimes, but I don't care enough for it to hanker after it.'

Sometimes Clemens' reinventions were shamelessly in pursuit of commercial profit. When he wrote *The Innocents Abroad*, Clemens urged his publisher to throw him a dinner to celebrate its success. Sam wouldn't attend the dinner. In fact, no-one would, so it wouldn't cost a penny. But the newspapers could reprint the speech and as a result the book would sell more.

This little fiction is what historian Daniel Boorstin later dubbed a 'pseudo event', a hollow occasion created only to be covered by the press. Clemens was a journalist who was obviously not troubled at crossing the lines of journalistic integrity, but such fictions were small compared with the grand fiction of his life as Mark Twain. To be sure, humorists of his time often used pseudonyms, but each name typically had a brief shelf life before the public tired of it. Preparing for Mark Twain's 'demise', Clemens even had a new name prepared: Carl Bying. But the success of Mark Twain took off and Clemens slowly grew into his alter ego.

Some biographers interpret 'Mark Twain' by saying that Sam Clemens needed this new persona because his own personality was larger than life. But others have pointed out the psychological insecurities behind it. One must have almost no identity, or at least deep insecurities, to live so completely as someone else. in fact, Clemens was always aware of the gap between his 'identity' and his 'image', his person and his pose, his real life and his publicly recounted life. His lifetime achievement was to turn the awkward and uncertain boy-man, Sam Clemens, into the assured, brilliant, witty public man of letters, Mark Twain. But there was a cost. Life for Twain was one grand performance with the world as his ever-present audience.

As an old man, Clemens wrote to his friend and fellow-writer William Dean Howells, 'You will never know how much enjoyment you have lost until you get to dictating your autobiography … And you will be astonished (& charmed) to see how like talk it is, & how real it sounds.' But he skilfully disguised the real truth of his life in a manner he noted in an earlier humorous piece, 'An Encounter with an Interviewer'. A reporter comes to interview Mark Twain, who responds with a blizzard of lies and contradictory details. Eventually, the reporter despairs of establishing the truth and settles for Twain's absurd but humorous tale. So long as the story entertains, it suggests, who cares about truth? Strict veracity is for pedants and governesses.

Face value

Where did the modern vogue for invention and reinvention come from? If an ideology is a set of ideas that serves as an intellectual weapon to advance social interests, the idea of a persona-as-propaganda is similar: the creative production of a personality to advance an agenda. In one sense both strategies are as old as the fall, and no-one highlighted the second more than Jesus of Nazareth in his celebrated attacks on 'hypocrisy'.

The word used for 'hypocrite' in the gospels is the normal Greek term for 'actor', but Jesus gave it the distinctive twist of moral deception that it still carries. To be sure, Machiavelli later reversed this disapproval, providing a legitimacy to deception and making it an essential weapon in statecraft. But only in the last century and a half has western society as a whole followed Machiavelli and reduced the importance of character to the vanishing point.

Ideas have played their part in this process, but social factors have been decisive – above all the impact of increasing mobility and the rise of a culture of image. Modern life has simultaneously shifted from the country to the city, from the supremacy of words to the primacy of images, and from relatively static, face-to-face relationships to mobile, fleeting superficial contacts. In the process there has been a parallel shift of emphasis from the internal to the external, and thus from the 'strong character' so prized by traditional society to the 'striking personality' and 'successful image' so touted today.

'If I had another face, do you think I would wear this one?' Abraham Lincoln's famous reply to Stephen Douglas's calling him two-faced shows the state of affairs at the time image-makeovers were not yet conceivable and the place of character was supreme. In the nineteenth century, the words of the British statesman George Canning were much quoted: 'My road must be through character to power; I will try no other course; and I am sanguine enough to believe that this course, though not perhaps the quickest, is the surest.' Today character would be viewed as the slow road to advancement, if not a handicap.

In a world in which first impressions may be the only impressions, we have to 'sell ourselves on sight'. In such a world of appearances, character loses significance, 'face value' becomes all important, and the door is opened to the 'makeover era' of spin-doctors and plastic surgeons.

Image-makeovers through lifestyle changes, facelifts, hair implants, creative CVs, and stage-managed confessions are all minted from the same coin.

A forty-five-year-old American cosmetic-surgery adviser gushed to London's *Sunday Times* about her ten-year 'marathon of surgery' in pursuit of new beauty (eyes, nose, chin, tummy, and knees, to start with): 'This is the real me. I felt like a misfit in my old face and body; it never felt right. This is the way I want to live, and I couldn't do it with my old face and body – I don't even associate myself with that person. She's dead. I cut her up.'

In Balzac's terms, we can all be kings and queens of invention, 'creating yourself a second time as if in mocking defiance of the Deity'. If 'your face is your fortune', as the advertisers claim, who can afford to look less than their best? As Erving Goffman argued in 1959 in *The Presentation of Self in Everyday Life*, life itself is theatre, we all spend our days on stage, we all live for effect, and we are all in the business of 'impression management'.

Curiously, even the findings of the evolutionary sciences are now being pressed into support of impression management. The female firefly in one species, we are told, mimics the mating flash of females in another and then, having attracted a male, eats him. Or again, some orchids look quite like female wasps in order to lure male wasps who will then spread their pollen. 'In short,' one proponent writes, 'natural selection's disdain for the principle of truth in advertising is widely evident … Organisms may present themselves as whatever it is in their interests to seem like.' As Richard Dawkins asserts in his foreword to *The Selfish Gene*, 'deceit is fundamental to animal communication'.

When the advocates of natural selection are adding their voices to the assault on truth it casts a curious light on the status of their own theories. Should we be hearing them as claims to truth or as a bid for power? And deeper still, do these proponents see human truth-seeking as underwritten and rewarded by the universe itself, or as a point of alienation from nature and a handicap in survival?

Nothing people

Clearly, Darwin's 'horrid doubt' is nagging worse than ever, but the erosion of truth caused by social forces is older and wider than the latest claims in evolutionary science. Put differently, character was traditionally understood as the inner form that makes anyone or anything what it is – whether a person, a wine, or a historical period. It is therefore deeper than, and different from, such outer concepts as personality, image, reputation, and celebrity. Character was the deep selfhood, the essential stuff a person is made of, the core reality in which thoughts, words, decisions, behaviour, and relationships are rooted. As such, character determined behaviour just as behaviour demonstrated character. Character was *who we are when no-one sees us – but God.*

All this changed dramatically in the twentieth century. The Russian notion of the 'nothing person' in the late nineteenth century and Robert Musil's novel *The Man Without Qualities* in Vienna before the First World War were early-warning signals of the crisis of selfhood and the dissolution of character. In a famous passage in Musil's novel, a couple are discussing a friend of theirs, Ulrich. Suddenly, the husband, Walter, bursts out: 'He is a man without qualities!'

'What's that?' Clarisse asked.

'Nothing. That's just the point – it's nothing!' And as

they discuss it further, he adds: 'There are millions of them nowadays. It's the human type our time has produced.'

Groping for words, Walter describes an emerging type of person who is all surface, skills, and CV – and no character. Today we would employ such descriptions as the 'empty suit', the 'designer personality', or the 'leader as panderer' who is a parade of poses, each one struck according to opinion polls and focus groups.

For example, *People* magazine reported that a celebrated multimillionaire business leader choked up while giving a speech to lay off some of his workforce. 'Afterward, everyone was debating whether he was faking it.' *People*'s own comment was: 'He's a man of disarming charm, his signature bow tie and his grin a little lopsided. The question is, is [his] warmth real or simply another designer choice?'

By the end of the twentieth century, Musil's new type had emerged strongly and it was widely accepted that old notions such as 'true self' had gone the way of commonsense reality. The new sense of 'empty' or 'decentred' self was chosen, not given or cultivated; it was shifting, not stable; and it was more in line with eastern views of the not-self than such solid western notions as human rights and human beings 'made in the image of God'.

The emphasis now is on surface, not depth; on possibilities, not qualities; on glamour, not convictions; on what can be altered endlessly, not achieved for good; and on what can be bought and worn, not gained by education and formation. To be a person is therefore to be a project. It is up to each of us to create and wear our own 'designer personality', carefully crafting ourselves with CVs, skills, and appearances all chosen with the expertise and care of a

Paris couturier designing a dress for a Hollywood actress on Oscar night. Character may be its own reward, but personality is what wins friends, gets jobs, attracts lovers, catches the camera's eye, and lands the prize of public office.

A young woman parading naked at the 1999 Burning Man Festival was exuberant with the freedom of the new self-invention. 'I can be free, I can be naked, I can be fat, I can be gay. You can just be whatever it is you need to be, today.' With all the possibilities offered by today's leisure and entertainment technologies, whether occasional festivals like Burning Man or the common person's escape via the imaginative role-playing bulletin boards of cyberspace, modern society has created an array of 'free-invention zones'. Enter one and you are only a choice (or click) away from being someone or something else.

Who needs a Concorde to whisk you to Paris or state troopers to procure you pleasures on the side when you are only a click away from a novel, psychic 'time out' that would be the envy of potentates and libertines of the past?

As Peter Berger observes, 'Dostoyevsky proposed that if God does not exist, everything is permitted. The proposition could be paraphrased: If God does not exist, any self is possible – and the question as to which of the many selves is "true" becomes meaningless.'

For some people, this experience is liberating; for others it creates anxiety. But, as postmodern people, all of us are schooled in the business of impression management and the glamour of surfaces. Like it or not, our task is to be unflagging impresarios creating our own images, tireless promoters putting on our own public shows. Everyone in public life today should be eligible for nomination for an Oscar. Truth and character are dead. We're all actors and spinmeisters now.

So the crisis of truth and character joins the crisis of truth and ethics. But drastic as they are, these two crises are only the foundation for the real harm of postmodernism: its damage to western civilization.

THREE

THE WEST
VERSUS ITSELF

Sweden's Uppsala has a well-deserved reputation as a historic and delightful city. Sometimes described as the 'Oxford or Harvard of Scandinavia', it boasts a distinguished university and beautiful surroundings. But for many visitors, the most fascinating part is Gamla Uppsala, the old Uppsala just outside the present town.

Set in rolling green fields, where waves once lapped, lie the remains of settlements that go back to at least 5000 BC. But three gigantic grassy mounds are the main attraction: the royal boat-graves of Viking kings from around AD 500 that are dedicated to Odin, the god of war, Thor, the god of thunder, and Frey, the god of fertility. Each grave holds remains of the royal warrior-chiefs along with their slaves, horses, weapons, and food, and each is a treasure of archaeological significance. The varied artefacts speak of the violent manliness of a terrifying bygone era so out of tune with the pastoral quiet of today's setting.

To one side of the boat-graves lies another historical

attraction – the site of the last pagan temple and the first Christian church in this region of Scandinavia. The Christian faith came late to this part of northern Europe, and evidently around AD 1100 the last temple and the first church were locked in spiritual conflict for about a hundred years. To anyone with historical imagination, the tension from this Scandinavian Mount Carmel is still palpable, a war of the worlds and worldviews, of the God of Sinai and Galilee against the gods of the pagan Vikings.

Then 'inevitably', as Christians might say without thinking, the Christian faith triumphed, the church prospered, and paganism receded from Sweden like a morning mist before the rising sun. But if I was thinking like that on my first visit, the guide soon snapped my reverie. 'Of course,' she said gaily, 'today the situation is reversed. The churches in Sweden are empty and paganism is on the rise.'

When I heard her words, I didn't need to be reminded of the statistics. In parts of the American upper Midwest where Scandinavians are strong, over 70% attend church regularly – well above the American average. But in Sweden itself, where nearly 98% of Swedes are formally Lutherans, fewer than 2% attend church. Nietzsche, it seems, was correct about Scandinavia: The 'death of God' is a reality of modern Swedish life.

What a difference a century makes. In AD 1900, the Christian faith, which was Asian and not European in origin, had become influential in only one continent and wherever that continent held sway – Europe. Then suddenly, a century later the Christian faith had become the world's 'first universal religion' and was present and growing on all five continents. Yet from one century to the next it had lost its dominance and much of its influence in Europe.

The guide's remark in Uppsala set off a train of thinking that accelerated when I read Samuel Huntington's celebrated 1993 essay (and later book), 'The Clash of Civilizations?' About the same time, I was visiting Singapore with my son and heard a Chinese economist give a Pacific Rim view of the world after the collapse of the Soviet Union. His statement was stunning and succinct: 'What we in Singapore want', he said, 'is the modern world, not the West. We want the Asian way, not the American way. We want to follow Confucius, not Christ.' He went on to explain, 'Having given rise to the modern world, the Jewish and Christian faiths have now been reduced to ruins by the modern world.' Asian countries, he argued, should take a different path. They should exploit the opportunities of capitalism, industrialized technology, and telecommunications, but within the setting of their own beliefs and cultures.

Asian confidence in 'Asian values' was somewhat dented by their own financial troubles in the late 1990s and its partial roots in cronyism. But the overall perspective of the economist and Samuel Huntington remain important. Talk of 'failed states' and the 'borderless world' of the new economy may be widespread, though the day of the nation-state is far from over. Yet the civilizational fault-lines in the world remain powerful and significant.

In Huntington's analysis, the Jewish and Christian roots of western civilization pit it against, say, the Buddhist and Confucian roots of Asia and the Islamic roots of the Middle East. Huntington therefore speaks of the clash of civilizations as 'the West versus the rest'. But James Kurth of Swarthmore College in the US has developed the discussion significantly. A closer look, he argues, shows that the situation is not as much 'the West versus the rest' but 'the West versus itself'.

That is, the West is unique in having an intellectual elite and cultural vanguard that are simultaneously secularist, tone-deaf toward the faiths of most ordinary citizens, and, at their most radical, openly dismissive of the roots of the civilization itself. Kurth writes of this elite, 'The fact of the matter is that Western civilization is the *only* civilization that is explicitly *non-religious* or post-religious. That is the radical difference of the West from the other civilizations … And it also points to a possible fatal flaw within Western civilization itself.'

Not just the obvious

For those who evaluate the present position of the West in light of the global challenges, the importance of post-modernism and its crisis of truth becomes plain, as we will explore further below. But its global significance is only one of several dimensions of postmodernism that is commonly overlooked.

Postmodernism is a movement and a mood as much as a clear set of ideas, so it often feels as if it is everywhere and nowhere. Doubtless, this means it is blamed for too much as well as too little. There are, of course, tell-tale fingerprints that postmodernism leaves on all it touches: the rejection of truth and objective standards of right and wrong, the levelling of authorities, the elevation of the autonomous self as the sole arbiter of life and reality, the equalizing of cultures, the promotion of image over character, the glorifying of power, the resort to victim-playing and identity politics, the licensing of victims' right to lie ('fibbing rights', as journalist Christopher Hitchens terms it), and so on.

Because of these obvious influences, observers have traced postmodernism's effect on various trends, ranging from sloppiness in dress ('The Age of No Class,' as the *Washington Post* has described it), to a serious coarsening of speech over the public airwaves, to a significant rise in scientific misconduct and fraud, to an increased 'literary licence' in journalism, to the new 'liberation marketing' in advertising, and to a troubling rise of misrepresentation and accounting gimmicks in business. Investor Warren Buffett warns, 'These managers often say that ... in using accounting shenanigans to get the figures they want, they are only doing what everyone else does. Once such an everybody's-doing-it attitude takes hold, ethical misgivings vanish.'

Undoubtedly, the most discussed trend is political correctness. Ironically, however, although many people debate, praise, or attack it, they miss the simplicity of its underlying dynamic. The phenomenon is the direct result of the dynamic of postmodernism, for when truth dies and power becomes the operative principle of speech, the result is conformity, the 'tyranny of consensus'.

Just as iron filings are drawn to the strongest magnet, so minds weakened by a loss of truth are drawn to the most powerful positions. As American legislator Sam Rayburn quipped in an earlier generation, 'When two men agree on everything, one of them is doing all the thinking.' The result is 'political correctness', a blend of bullying, conformity, and hypocrisy that makes all opinions equal but some more equal than others.

And irony of ironies, political correctness is a direct child of the 1960s that hated such conformity. Ken Kesey's name for the tyranny of consensus was the 'Combine', and what he attacked so effectively in his novel *One Flew Over the Cuckoo's Nest* was exactly the smooth workings of the consensus-controlling Combine.

Outside political correctness, the postmodern position

is often at its noisiest and most pretentious in literary theory, with its bid to replace philosophy as the arbiter of meaning and its vociferous attacks on the canon and 'dead white European males'. And it is at its most dangerous in legal theory, because of its power to debunk and subvert such foundational notions as 'the rule of law', 'trial by jury', 'evidence', 'swearing on oath', and 'perjury'. Law is reduced to 'power games' and a battle of 'dream-team lawyers'.

As the infamous acquittals in the O. J. Simpson trial and US President Clinton's impeachment illustrate, 'lawyered truth' is anything you can say and make stick in a court of law so long as you don't fall foul of ethics rules and perjury charges. So the Simpson trial was made into a national referendum on American racism and the Clinton impeachment a national referendum on the same country's broad-mindedness about sex.

In each case, truth and justice could be shouldered aside in the process. And the tactic was deliberate. Paul Butler, an American law professor, states the general position clearly. He believes that his country's legal system is irreparably racist, so he counsels openly that in non-violent drug cases, 'The black juror ought to use her power to emancipate the brother, even if he is absolutely 100% guilty.'

But we would also be wise to trace the impact of postmodernism beyond these obvious levels. This chapter therefore examines its effect at three often overlooked places: the global level, in indirect ways, and through the special influence of powerful 'gatekeeping' individuals.

From 'Great Experiment' to 'permanent revolution'

How has the postmodern movement influenced affairs globally just as decisively as locally? As we saw in the introduction, the transition from modernism to post-modernism is a watershed moment for western civilization and its leadership, particularly as epitomized in America's dominance, and potentially decisive for the future of both.

It can be argued, I think convincingly, the story of the West is a movement with three phases. Phase one was Christendom, a long and explicitly religious period that was ended by the Enlightenment in the eighteenth century. Since then, the intellectual class has never in large numbers returned to faith. Phase two was 'European civilization', Christendom's secularized successor that co-incided with Europe's rise to world prominence; it ended with Europe's exhaustion and disillusionment after the First World War. Phase three, from 1918 to the present, is America's leadership of the West. With the American Creed providing the faith, the West in its New World form eventually prevailed in vast global struggles (such as the two world wars and the Cold War) and has carried its ideals and way of life to every part of the earth.

The question now, of course, is 'Where is America's leadership of the West?' In addressing the situation we need to look back to the American framers. Seeing how the modernism of the Enlightenment was in tension with the traditions of Christendom, they married what earlier and elsewhere were considered incompatible: republican-ism and religion. The result was not only a unique ordering of religion and public life that provided a central source of national vitality; the new union also smoothed the tensions between tradition and modernism that had so often convulsed Europe.

The emergence of postmodernism shattered that equilibrium. Today postmodern sceptics repudiate the Christian faith, the Enlightenment, and the idea of the West with equal force. To the extent that postmodernism has penetrated the intellectual elite, the idea of the American experiment has been altered and the idea of the West itself has been abandoned.

For the framers, what George Washington called the 'Great Experiment' meant the testing, and therefore confirming or disproving, of a specific, well-defined hypothesis about ordered liberty. Far more than winning freedom successfully, the so-called 'new science of politics' was about ordering and sustaining it. Theirs was an audacious attempt to use history in order to defy history and break what the Greeks and Romans saw as 'the natural cycle of constitutional revolutions' by which republics rise and fall.

For the postmodernists, by contrast, there is no need for order, only liberty. Experiment therefore means open-ended experimentation. Nothing is fixed, everything is fluid and free; nothing is given, everything is up for grabs. Current management consultants buzz excitedly about the ceaseless remaking, reinventing, restructuring, and re-engineering of corporations. And left-wing intellectuals speak similarly of endless social reinventing en route to what postmodern philosopher Richard Rorty calls 'achieving our country'.

The theoretical result is a view of America closer to Leon Trotsky's 'permanent revolution' than the framers' experiment in ordered liberty. And the practical result is even worse: if everything is endlessly open to question and change, then everything is permitted, nothing is forbidden, and literally nothing is unthinkable. Considering the character of the republic set up by the framers, the long-term outcome of postmodernism can only be America's decline. The only question is when – and how much chaos, evil, and suffering will accompany it.

The postmodern assault on the idea of America's leadership of the West is even stronger. Many intellectuals in the United States care nothing for their country's role as 'defender of the faith' for the West. Some no longer view the role as legitimate, arguing that the United States is now truly multicultural and not western. Others go further still and attack the role as illegitimate. To them, western civilization is an 'oppressive hegemony' as violent to the peoples of the world as the slave-owning framers of the American 'Experiment' have been to Native Americans, African Americans, and women as a whole.

James Kurth's conclusion about this postmodern assault is sobering. At the very least, he writes, it 'has already succeeded in marginalizing Western civilization in its very intellectual core, the universities and the media of America'. More seriously still, the triumph of the postmodern over the modern also means the overthrow of the western by the post-western:

> At the very moment of its greatest triumph, its defeat of the last great power opposing it, Western civilization is becoming non-Western … The real clash of civilizations will not be between the West and one or more of the rest. It will be between the West and the post-West, within the West itself.

What bringing it in brings in

A second commonly overlooked point of postmodern influence is hugely important. Those who look only for the direct impact of postmodernism miss a vital dimension: its indirect influence. For just as the Greeks entered Troy concealed in the hollow wooden statue of a horse, so postmodernism is providing the cover for all sorts of ideas and practices to enter western life – ideas that on their own would have difficulty gaining entrance.

A clear example of the Trojan-horse effect is health care. Advances in medicine and medical practices, especially immunization and antibiotics, were among the most stunning accomplishments of the twentieth century. For instance, worldwide life expectancy increased from forty-five years in 1900 to seventy-five by the century's end. Yet curiously, the year 2000 saw such triumphs under attack and western medicine in a defensive position against alternative medicine, including fringe remedies and treatments.

To be sure, scientific medicine today shows many of the weaknesses of modernism: it is justly criticized for being professionalized, commercialized, 'secularized', 'techni-cized', depersonalized, and so forth. But for all its limitations, western medicine would hardly be overthrown for practices that only recently were considered super-stition were it not for postmodernism.

Two examples of alternative medicine that are making deep inroads into health care are *Ayurvedic* medicine, championed by Deepak Chopra, and Therapeutic Touch with its notions of a 'personal energy field'. Both have a strong, openly religious dimension and trace their ideas back to Hinduism. Dr Chopra learned *Ayurveda* (the 'science of life') from the Maharishi Mahesh Yogi, guru to the Beatles, who in turn pronounced him 'Dhanvantari (Lord of Immortality), the keeper of perfect health for the world'. Public broadcasting seems only slightly less impressed.

Of course, postmodernism is not responsible for the content of the new ideas; it acts, however, as a Trojan horse bringing Hinduism into western medicine by providing a sense of plausibility. It does so in two ways. On the one hand, it *softens the rational criteria of investigation.* The result of its assault on truth and reason is to replace objective, experimental, scientific data with personal, anecdotal experience.

On the other hand, postmodernism *hardens political considerations.* For example, scientific rejection of altern-ative medicine as 'unscientific' is itself rejected with the countercharge that science is 'patriarchal' and medicine is a 'mechanistic, male domination of female-oriented nursing'. 'Diversity' and 'academic freedom' are then appealed to as grounds for including any therapy 'that works'. One mainstream nursing textbook recommends Therapeutic Touch with just this argument: 'Therapeutic Touch is rooted in Eastern philosophy … To the Eastern mind, if it works, one doesn't research to prove how it works. The Eastern mind doesn't care how it works, only that it does.'

Such attitudes raise a cluster of issues, from the significance of eastern religion for foundational western ideals to the dangers to public health. The underlying point, however, is plain: postmodernism is like the Trojan horse. Bring it in and you bring in a lot more too. 'Beware Greeks bearing gifts' is as apt today as to the Trojans long ago. Postmodernism opens the door and ushers in an assortment of the weird, the wild, and the wonderful, with no questions asked or allowed.

The 'corruptingest' president of all

A third commonly overlooked point of postmodern influence is its influence on western society through significant gatekeepers, supremely, given America's dominance, the president of the United States. 'If President Clinton didn't exist, he would have to be invented.' Several times in interviews during the Clinton/Lewinsky scandal I opened the discussion with this comment, and with apologies to Voltaire. In other words, the crisis was not just the sad story of a brilliant but deeply flawed political leader, but the full flowering of a generation of trends in society. On the one hand, the American president was fully responsible for what he did. On the other, he represented and reinforced the wider developments around him that become culturally potent because of his gatekeeping position and power as president.

Bill Clinton was often described as the first baby-boomer president. More significantly, he was also the first postmodern American president – not only the first president in the postmodern era, but the first president himself to be postmodern through and through. The Lewinsky affair is therefore an excellent gauge by which to assess the impact of postmodernism on American politics and law. In terms of the standing of truth in the American republic, the scandal represents the postmodern crisis of truth in presidential form: America's 'Nietzschean moment' in the Oval Office; the year America learned to live with the lie.

The Clinton/Lewinsky scandal became a profound crisis for truth in American public life as a trio of forces converged: a virtuoso liar of a president; his morally contorted supporters from his fellow-Democrats to his wife, who in their support for him enabled him and demeaned themselves; and a largely confused and complacent public willing to become complicit in their own corruption.

The first and most important force was the deliberate, repeated, and pervasive lying of the president himself under oath before the law. He lied to his wife, his friends, his staff, his lawyers, his cabinet, the congressional leaders, and the American people. 'Clinton's an unusually good liar,' Democratic Senator Bob Kerrey said. According to Monica Lewinsky, the president admitted that he had been a serial liar since childhood. Monica herself confessed separately, 'I have lied my entire life.' Clearly Bill and Monica's relationship was a liaison of liars.

Scholars have described Clinton as 'the most skilful liar in American presidential history', and journalists have come up with a host of words to describe him: his 'want of truth', his 'fluid conception of what's real', his 'situational veracity', his 'believing everything he says when he says it', and the like. One of the earliest bumper stickers skewered his lying perfectly: 'Bill Clinton: 99% Fact-free!'

Seven habits of postmodern lying

It is important, however, to see not just the individual lies of the scandal but the wider postmodern features that amplify their plausibility. These may be described as the seven habits of highly effective postmodern lying.

Pride of mind. With postmodernism teaching that truth is 'created, not discovered', the premium on the 'best and brightest' increases and the prize becomes the triumph of intellect over reality. How else could those 'first in their class' at Georgetown, Oxford, and Yale think they could unravel the knottiest problems of the nation and the world simply by throwing their minds at them? How could they, by their own fiat, declare themselves in advance 'the most ethical administration in the history of the Republic'? By all accounts there was little tragic sense of history in the Clinton administration.

Partitioning. With pluralism, fragmentation, time-pressure, overload of choice, and 'multitasking' at the heart of postmodern life, a natural result is psychological and social partitioning. We not only wear different hats; we are tempted to have different souls.

'Compartmentalizing' was the US president's word for cordoning off the unpleasant realities in his life. His characteristic resort to it led to CNN's term 'the split-screen presidency' and to a leading journalist's damning description of the 'Jekyll and Hyde' personalities of the 'Sunday morning president' (or 'daylight Clinton') and 'Saturday night Bill' (or 'Clinton noir').

People-pleasing. Described variously as 'other-directedness' and 'outside-in thinking', the inordinate desire to please people is a characteristic of the postmodern personality. Likewise, skill in doing so is a common source of power in postmodern leadership. 'Don't be fooled by the president's gratitude to you,' I was told after a session at Camp David discussing the State of the Union address. 'He is whom he speaks to last.'

Similarly, one close advisor wrote, 'While many people tap into an internal energy source, often spiritual, Clinton derives his stimulation only externally, from his environment. In this respect, he is more like a roadside reflector than a car's headlight ... As a result, he craves stimulation. He cannot stand his own emptiness when left in solitude. He lives from high to high.' Or as America's *New Republic* commented, 'Like a Visa card, he is everywhere you want him to be.' Even the First Lady described her husband's weakness as the consequence of his being caught as a four-year-old between his mother and grandmother: 'There is always the desire to please each one.'

Posturing. The postmodern apparatus of 'impression management' is not unique to the Clinton administration, but rarely has it been used so effectively in the interests of a purely personal, shabby affair. Examples of mendacious posturing are among the most enduring images of Clinton's presidency: the First Couple's much publicized embrace on a Caribbean beach when he knew the scandal would break only a few days later; the regulation hand-holding on entering and exiting the presidential heli-copter; the large-sized Bible flourished en route to church (and en route to a Sunday liaison with his lover); the square-jawed, finger-wagging denial of impropriety to the American people; the catch-in-the-voice 'I honour her,' saluting his betrayed wife in the Congressional gallery; even the macho *Wag the Dog* launching of Cruise missiles against a falsely described factory in Sudan. As the Reverend Jesse Jackson said of Clinton in 1992, 'There's *nothing* he won't do. He's immune to shame. Move past all the nice posturing and get really down in there in him, you find absolutely nothing ... nothing but an appetite.'

Prevarication. Acting and speaking evasively is as old as human deceitfulness, but if truth is dead and knowledge is power, postmodernism is the philosophy of choice for a prevaricator. Bill Clinton has trailed quibbles and equi-vocations behind him at every phase of his public life. He 'never broke the drug laws of [his] country' (just Britain's; he was overseas). He didn't 'inhale' marijuana. He didn't have 'sexual relations with that woman'; it all 'depends on how you define "*alone*"' (he meant he wasn't alone in the entire White House) or 'what the meaning of the word *is* is.' He didn't coach his secretary to give false testimony, only to refresh his memory.

When Clinton defended himself against his reputation for weasel-wording and 'parsing words too closely', America's *Washington Post* translated it with brutal plainness: 'toying with truth'. Journalist Joe Klein called it 'lawyering the truth'. Even the president's own counsel testified that a reasonable person might well conclude that the president had lied under oath. Again the *Washington Post* was blunt. Describing the president's response to the articles of impeachment as 'tortured argumentation' and 'the same old legalistic hair-splitting', it concluded: 'It is difficult to find a single honest sentence in the factual defense of the perjury charge.' When Lanny Davis, one of the president's scandal spokesmen, defended him on ABC'S *Nightline*, his son Seth told him: 'Dad, even I know that you know you are full of crap.'

Power-plays. For first-hand witnesses of the Lewinsky scandal and those who followed it in the press, illustrating the postmodern emphasis on power would be redundant. The Clinton impeachment was the O. J. Simpson trial of politics, and his tactic of 'brazening out scandal' is among his poisoned legacies: 'I never did it. What's your problem with it anyway? And it's time to move on/get back to the people's business/secure my place in history.' Certainly, one of the most quoted presidential statements was Clinton's response upon hearing the results of a poll. Voters were willing to forgive the president for adultery but not for perjury or obstruction of justice. 'Well,' Clinton replied, 'we just have to win then.' Or as White House staffer Paul Begala put it, the first rule of politics is: 'Define and create the reality you want.'

If law itself, in the language of postmodernism, is 'an instrument of social, economic, and political domination', then the philosophy is clear: he who has the highest polls, the best dream-team lawyers, the most ferocious attack-dog consultants, and the most tirelessly ingenious spinmeisters wins. Real men seize power.

Personalizing. A well-known feature of postmodernism is its stress on 'story' at the expense of 'propositional truth', an overemphasis that translates into politics as the personalizing of issues. The old adage 'All politics is local' becomes 'All politics is personal'. Thus speeches become self-referential, close supporters are 'friends of Bill', White House staffers leave because of 'personal betrayal' rather than resigning on principle, and in a grotesque twist even the impeachment becomes a point of personal pride. Speaking to an interviewer after it was over, the president said he felt 'honoured' to have had a chance to defend the Constitution by warding off impeachment. So 'I do not regard this impeachment vote as some great badge of shame'.

Not over yet

The year after his impeachment President Clinton was guest of honour at the White House correspondents' dinner in Washington, DC. Impeached, fined for being in contempt of court, facing possible disbarment, exposed as a brazen womanizer and shameless liar, accused publicly of sexual harassment, thuggery, and rape, the president took the dinner's tradition of self-parody to a shameless extreme. He joked that his disgrace did not even make the top fifty in a recent list of the twentieth century's top hundred stories. 'I don't mind telling you I made the list …' Clinton said. 'Number fifty-three. Fifty-three? I mean, what does a guy have to do to make the top fifty around here?'

'Moving on' and 'making light of it' – Clinton was relying on two stock contemporary substitutes for repentance and moral resolution. But not so fast. Devastating high-level damage of the sort he inflicted on his nation cannot be removed with a wave of the wand. President Clinton's credibility at home is virtually zero and the credibility of the presidency has been severely weakened. Only a solid succession of presidents with character and integrity will decisively repudiate Clinton's dishonest style and re-establish the standards of the American founders.

So what does this 'Nietzschean moment' of America mean? Some lamented it, saying that it spelled the defeat of the conservatives in the culture war. Others hailed it, claiming that Clinton's greatest legacy was his defeat of conservatives and the religious right. But in one of the deepest commentaries, the impeachment acquittal was called America's 'Dreyfus case', the false acquittal that revealed the rottenness in its institutions just as the false conviction of Alfred Dreyfus had exposed the rottenness in France in 1893. 'Deceit at the highest levels. A verdict that ignores the facts. A verdict rationalized because a revered institution must be protected. Popular approval of the verdict. A disdained minority protesting it.' And then of course history's unravelling of the lies, a reversal of public opinion, and an overturning of the verdict.

My own analysis is similar. Far more than a 'mistake', a private lapse, a limited partisan skirmish, or a Republican payback for Watergate, the Clinton/Lewinsky affair and the impeachment verdict were a breakthrough for post-modernism at the political and legal levels, revealing the depth of America's crisis of truth.

If such developments are not reversed but tie in with the consequences of postmodernism in other spheres of society, America's crisis of cultural authority will have gathered pace, its framers' vision of the American experiment will have been superseded, America's current leadership of the West will be jeopardized, and President Clinton will have proved not just one of the most corrupt but the most corrupting president in its history. As Adlai Stevenson warned a generation ago, 'those who corrupt the public mind are just as evil as those who steal from the public purse'.

Carelessness the West can ill afford

Unquestionably, the assaults on truth, ethics, and character that we've explored raise complicated issues, but can anyone doubt the seriousness of the consequences? Heraclitus told his fellow-Greeks that they must fight for their laws and customs as determinedly as for their city walls. Americans today, however, combine a capacity to rain down Cruise missiles on foreign lands with a carelessness that hardly bothers about the underminers of their laws and customs – including those who rain down missiles on foreign lands.

'We hold these truths to be self-evident,' Thomas Jefferson trumpeted in the Declaration of Independence. But two centuries later the trumpet is silent. Few things are less self-evident and more alienable in contemporary America than truth of any kind. As philosopher Alasdair MacIntyre asserts bluntly in light of modern philosophy, 'there are no self-evident truths'. Confidence in natural rights is comparable to 'belief in witches and unicorns'.

Vaporized by critical theories, twisted by ideologies, hollowed out and replaced by psychological categories, obscured by clouds of euphemism and jargon, outpaced by rumour and hype, softened by mawkish sentiment parading as emotion, truth in America today is anything but marching on. Its citizens have reached the place, says art historian Robert Hughes, where they appear to 'want to create a sort of linguistic Lourdes where evil and misfortune are dispelled by a day in the waters of euphemism'.

We are told that in the weeks before Thomas Jefferson's death on 4 July 1826, he invited all his grandchildren to Monticello and urged them each to 'pursue virtue, be true and truthful'. Truth, he saw with twilight clarity, was essential to freedom. Yet as one historian observes, Jefferson's belief that 'Truth is great and will prevail' (an old Irish saying) is today 'more a prayer than an axiom'. Much closer to the present state of affairs is Mort Sahl's famous quip in the Reagan era: 'George Washington couldn't tell a lie. Richard Nixon couldn't tell the truth. And the present occupant of the White House can't tell the difference.'

FOUR

DIFFERENCES MAKE A DIFFERENCE

Prisoner 174517 was thirsty. Seeing a fat icicle hanging just outside his hut in the Auschwitz extermination camp, he reached out of the window and broke it off to quench his thirst. But before he could get the icicle to his mouth, a guard snatched it out of his hands and dashed it into pieces on the filthy ground.

'Warum?' the prisoner burst out instinctively. 'Why?'

'Hier ist kein warum,' the guard answered with brutal finality. 'Here there is no why.'

That, for Primo Levi, the Italian Jewish scientist and writer, was the essence of the death camps: places not only of unchallengable, arbitrary authority but of absolute evil that defied all explanation. In the face of such wickedness, explanations born of psychology, sociology, and economics were pathetic in their inadequacy. One could only shoulder the weight of such an experience and bear witness to the world. 'Never again' was too confident an assertion. 'You never know' was the needed refrain.

Yet despite the horror, Levi gave the impression that he had survived the poison of Auschwitz and had come to terms with his nightmarish experience. One of only three returning survivors of the 650 Italian Jews transported to Poland in 1944, he eventually married, had children, wrote books, won literary prizes, and lived a full life. His core mission, however, was always to serve as a witness to the truth, a guardian of the memory.

Writing about his deportation to Poland, he stated: 'Auschwitz left its mark on me, but it did not remove my desire to live. On the contrary; that experience increased my desire, it gave my life a purpose, to bear witness, so that such a thing should never occur again.' While other direct or indirect victims of the Nazis committed suicide, including Walter Benjamin, Stefan Zweig, and Bruno Bettelheim, Levi many times argued against that act.

Thus many people were shocked and saddened when on 11 April 1987, more than forty years after his release from Auschwitz, Primo Levi plunged to his death down the stairwell of his home in Torino, Italy. Feeling the burden of witnessing, the guilt of surviving, the horror of revisionist denials of the camps, the weariness of repeating the same things, and even the anxiety of seeing his own memories fade, he joined the long sad list of the victims of the Nazi hell who took their own lives.

Levi's mounting depression in the last weeks of his life was known to his family and friends. Significantly, in his last interview he begged the questioning journalist not to consider him a prophet: 'Prophets are the plague of today, and perhaps of all time, because it is impossible to tell a true prophet from a false one.' In the same vein he had said earlier, 'All prophets are false. I don't believe in prophets, even though I come from a heritage of prophets.'

Prophets the 'plague of all time'? Levi's dismissal is understandable, for he was an atheist who had been to hell on earth and back. But it is sad, for the strong line of Hebrew prophets is not only a defining feature of his people's heritage but one of the richest Jewish gifts to the history of the world. Elijah, Elisha, Isaiah, Jeremiah, Amos, Hosea, and many others – each was a hero of the moral word whose 'Thus says the Lord' shattered the status quo of his day. They each opened up perspectives on God's truth, justice, and peace that restored the world, moved it forward through a transcendent point of leverage, or simply drew a line in the sand to mark off evil.

The prophetic calling, however, was closed to Levi because in his universe he acknowledged no caller. Unlike Søren Kierkegaard with his questing 'knight of faith', Levi recognized no higher majesty to dub him knight.

The weight of witness

It is often said that to have a fulfilling life, three essentials are required: a clear sense of personal identity, a deep sense of faith and meaning, and a strong sense of purpose and mission. Levi, it turned out, had a critical deficiency of the second and third, and in ways that poignantly illustrate our contemporary crisis of truth.

To all appearances, Primo Levi *did* have a clear sense of identity and a passionate sense of purpose. 'It is very likely', he said, 'that without Auschwitz I would never have written, and would have given only little weight to my Jewish identity.' But following Auschwitz, 'My only thought was to survive and tell.' Because of his desperate desire to tell his story to everyone he met, he would compare himself to Coleridge's ancient mariner, who pestered the wedding guests.

Levi's most telling testimony can be read at Auschwitz itself. In 1980 the Polish government restructured the design of the camp and asked Levi to introduce the Italian section. Of the eight paragraphs he submitted, only the last one stands there today:

VISITOR, OBSERVE THE REMAINS OF THIS CAMP AND CONSIDER: WHATEVER COUNTRY YOU COME FROM, YOU ARE NOT A STRANGER. ACT SO THAT YOUR JOURNEY IS NOT USELESS, AND OUR DEATHS NOT USELESS. FOR YOU AND YOUR SONS, THE ASHES OF AUSCHWITZ HOLD A MESSAGE. ACT SO THAT THE FRUIT OF HATRED, WHOSE TRACES YOU HAVE SEEN HERE, BEARS NO MORE SEED, EITHER TOMORROW OR FOR EVER AFTER.

What was it that undid Levi's mission to witness? The first and more obvious reason was philosophical. Levi lacked any sense of faith and meaning with which to interpret and handle his harrowing experience. An atheist when he went to Auschwitz, he could never get round the extermination camp as the black hole of godlessness, the extreme situation of absolute evil to which no response could ever be adequate.

For a time in 1944 he was struck by words from Dante's *Inferno*: 'Consider what you came from ... You were not born to live like mindless brutes.' This hit him 'like the blast of a trumpet, like the voice of God'. Two years later, in freedom and on meeting his wife, he felt he had at last found a place in the universe where it no longer appeared 'that the world was God's error'.

But in the end, the dark combination of Auschwitz and atheism always closed back in on him. For instance, in 1946 Levi described his raging in silence at an old Jew who thanked God for having escaped selection to the gas chambers: 'If I was God, I would spit at Kuhn's prayer.' Or as he stated more bluntly in his first book, *If This Is a Man*, 'If there is an Auschwitz, then there cannot be a God.' Forty years later, only months before his suicide, he wrote after those words in pencil: 'I find no solution to the riddle. I seek, but I do not find it.'

The second and less obvious reason for Levi's crisis was practical. He gradually realized that his mission, however noble and necessary, was impossible. As Liliane Atlan wrote in *An Opera for Theresientstadt*, Auschwitz is 'an experience both impossible to pass on, and impossible to forget'.

Most of the reasons for this difficulty are straight-forward. Memories are tricky and eventually fade. Revisionists who deny history are shocking, but are neither driven nor answered by facts. Besides, most people would rather not be reminded of evil of such magnitude. Then, too, generations pass and the new world of entertainment treats evil as fantasy.

Levi, for example, was amused but stunned when a ten-year-old schoolboy solemnly told him he should have cut a guard's throat and switched off the power to the electric fence, and then urged him not to forget this advice should he find himself in the same situation again.

But the weight of the witness was always heavier on Levi than the sum of the problems. 'We felt the weight of centuries on our shoulders,' he wrote. And the heaviest burden of all was the guilt of surviving – 'the best had been murdered' – along with the awful knowledge that confession was impossible, and yet without genuine confession there could be no real confrontation with evil. In the words of Itzhak Schipper, one of the 'murdered best' killed in Majdanek in 1943: 'No-one will want to believe us, because our disaster is the disaster of the entire civilized world.'

Finally, there was the agony of realizing that the ranks of the witnesses were thinning. 'We are many (but every year our numbers diminish) ...' Levi wrote. 'If we die in silence as our enemies desire ... the world will not learn what man could do and what he can still do.'

In a sense, Levi wrote at the end of his life, the hopelessness he was experiencing was worse than Auschwitz. For he was no longer young. The task of repeating the story was getting harder and harder. The burden of the witness was impossible. The way forward was hopeless. There was no other way out.

In the steps of Sisyphus

Obviously no suicide ever returns to speak of his or her death, and Levi left no note, so we must pause in respect. But it is almost impossible to read Levi's last interviews and writings without thinking of Albert Camus and the myth of Sisyphus. In classical legend, Sisyphus was condemned by Zeus to push a huge stone up the hill only to have it roll down again each time – a story that Camus used to picture human fate in a world without God and without meaning.

For those who find themselves without faith in God and who conclude that the world they desire does not fit with the world they discover, life is fundamentally deaf to their aspirations. And in fact, it is literally *absurd*. All meaning – including for Levi, the establishment of truth – is up to them. They must live so as to be able to say, in Nietzsche's words, 'Thus I have willed it.' Or as Frank Sinatra put it simply, 'I did it my way.'

So Levi must roll his 'truth' up the hill again and again.

When the vast indifference of the public makes the gradient steeper, he must push harder. When he rests for a moment and the revisionists shove his stone back down, he must start again. When his companions drop out and his energy flags, he must summon his strength one more time. Numb, exhausted, aching, despairing, he must roll it and roll it until he can roll it no more. In an absurd world no success will ever crown his labours with significance. He can have only one satisfaction: the rebel's reward of rolling, rolling, rolling, without end.

But there is an alternative to the fate of Sisyphus – and of Nietzsche, Camus, Sinatra, and Levi. It is that truth, like meaning as a whole, is not for to us to create but for us to discover. Each of us may be small, our lives short, and our influence puny. But if truth is there – objective, absolute, independent of minds that know it – then we may count on it and find it a source of strength.

Another victim of totalitarian evil stood on this solid ground beyond himself as he declared, 'One word of truth outweighs the entire world.' Solzhenitsyn with his statement had not suddenly outpowered the Soviets with some self-generated 'truth'. Rather, outpowered, outnumbered, and outgunned, he as one single person seized and wielded truth as a sword that could not be resisted, crying out, 'Grant, O Lord, that I may not break as I strike.'

Primo Levi and Aleksandr Solzhenitsyn were both witnesses to the horrors they experienced. They were both spurred on by their passion not to betray the dying wish of millions to be remembered. But whereas Levi's view of truth left him a weary Sisyphus with a hopeless task, Solzhenitsyn's made him a sword in God's hand and allowed him to raise a voice to rally the world. 'It is infinitely difficult to begin', he wrote in *The Oak and the Calf*, 'when mere words must remove a great block of inert matter. But there is no other way if none of the material strength is on your side. And a shout in the mountains has been known to start an avalanche.'

What am I arguing? Let me underscore it again. I am not countering the postmodern view of truth on behalf of the modern. One is as bad as the other; the postmodern is the direct descendant of the modern and the mirror image of its deficiencies. It is the more dangerous today only because it is more current. Nor am I raising purely theoretical arguments against the postmodern view of truth, for few people outside universities follow the complexities of the higher academic debates.

Rather, I am deliberately underscoring the practical difficulties that grow out of the theoretical deficiencies of the new radical relativism. We can easily be cowed into submission by the force or fashionability of new ideas without realizing their disastrous practical consequences for ordinary life. When that happens, the full answer to the problem in question must always include the theoretical answer. But practical arguments are an important first step in confronting the crisis.

With the present crisis of truth, practical arguments are vital in addressing two particular groups of people. One is those who hold to traditional Jewish and Christian assumptions about truth but have grown careless or hesitant in defending it. The other is those who do not hold to those beliefs but who care deeply about the society in which they live and the quality of their own lives in it. For each group, there are two powerful arguments for the practical importance of objective, non-relativist truth. As the contrast between Primo Levi and Aleksandr Solzhenitsyn shows, differences between views of truth, far from being purely theoretical and irrelevant, make an enormous difference.

Red-blooded truth

For those who hold to traditional biblical assumptions of truth but are uncertain whether they are worth defending, two arguments for the importance of a high view of truth stand out, one lesser and one greater.

The lesser argument is that without truth we cannot answer the fundamental objection that faith in God is simply a form of 'bad faith' or 'poor faith'. The wilder accusation of 'bad faith' comes from outside the Jewish and Christian communities and is one of the deepest and most damaging charges against these faiths in the last two centuries. Jews and Christians believe, critics say, not because of good reasons but because they are afraid not to believe. Without faith, they would be naked to the alternatives, such as the terror of meaninglessness or the nameless dread of unspecified guilt. Faith is therefore a handy shield to ward off the fear, a comforting tune to whistle in the darkness; it is, however, fundamentally untrue, irrational, and illegitimate – and therefore 'unauthentic' and 'bad faith'.

In modern times the charge of 'bad faith' was raised by the French existentialists, but is more widely associated with Marxist and Freudian attacks on religion. Religion for Marx was the 'opium of the people' and for Freud a 'projection'. Needless to say, the germ of the charge is far older and wider. 'Fear made the gods,' wrote Lucretius as a first-century BC Roman. Or as Henrik Ibsen remarked as a nineteenth-century Norwegian, 'Take away the life-lie from the average man and you take away his happiness.'

Whatever the historical period, the dynamic of the accusation is the same. As Aldous Huxley set it out more patiently,

Man inhabits, for his own convenience, a homemade universe within the greater alien world of external matter and his own irrationality. Out of the illimitable blackness of the world the light of his customary thinking scoops, as it were, a little illuminated cave – a tunnel of brightness, in which, from the brink of consciousness to its death, he lives, moves, and has his being ... We ignore the outer darkness; or if we cannot ignore it, if it presses too insistently upon us, we disapprove of being afraid.

There are several possible responses to this charge: for instance, those who wield it are rarely courageous enough to turn it on their own beliefs; the very charge is itself the biblical critique of idols; and so on. But at the end of the day, there is no answer without one: those who put their faith in God do so for all sorts of good reasons, but the very best reason is that they are finally, utterly, and incontrovertibly convinced that the faith in which they put their confidence is *true*.

'What is truth?' someone will immediately ask. Let me answer straightforwardly. In the biblical view, truth is that which is ultimately, finally, and absolutely real, or the 'way it is', and therefore is utterly trustworthy and dependable, being grounded and anchored in God's own reality and truthfulness. But this stress on the personal foundation of truth is not, as in postmodernism, at the expense of the propositional. Both accuracy and authenticity are important to truth.

If, in our ordinary speech, telling the truth is 'telling it like it is', we can say that *a statement, an idea, or a belief is true if what it is about is as it is presented in the statement*. Belief in something doesn't make it true; only truth makes a belief true. But without truth, a belief may be only speculation plus sincerity. Or perhaps, worse still, bad faith. A sardonic nineteenth-century wit once suggested that three words be carved in stone over all church doors: 'Important if true.' To which the Christian would reply, 'Important *because* true.'

The milder accusation, the parallel dismissal of faith as 'poor faith', comes from inside the church and is less serious but more common. Whereas both the Bible and the best thinkers of Christian history invite seekers to put their faith in God because the message conveying that invitation is true, countless Christians today believe for various other reasons. For instance, they believe faith is true 'because it works' (pragmatism), because they 'feel it is true in their experience' (subjectivism), because they sincerely believe it is 'true for them' (relativism), and so on.

For some of these Christians, the deficiency comes from bad teaching. For others, the motive is escape. Retreating into the fortress of personal experience, they can pull up the drawbridge of faith and feel impregnable to reason. But for all of them the outcome is a sickly faith deprived of the rude vigour of truth.

Tendencies toward this schizophrenic split between faith and reason have been evident since the Enlightenment, aided by such philosophers as Spinoza, who argued that 'Revelation and Philosophy stand on totally different footings', each with its own separate province. Earlier still, in the thirteenth century, the idea led to the disastrous medieval notion of 'double truth', according to which there are two truths, one for the supernatural world and one for the natural. Each was separate and contradictory, but the doubleness meant that the church could be right in theology while wrong in philosophy or science. Faith, in other words, was true even if it was nonsense. Believers could believe with their theological minds while disbelieving with their scientific minds.

Biblical faith, by contrast with both medieval and modern deficiencies, has a robust view of truth. All truth is God's truth and is true everywhere, for everyone, under all conditions. Truth is true in the sense that it is objective and independent of the mind of any human knower. Being true, it cannot contradict itself.

Human beliefs and truth-claims, in contrast, may be relative because we humans are finite. Therefore all beliefs are partial and provisional. But truth, guaranteed by God, is quite different. Created by God, not us, it is partly discovered and partly disclosed. It is singular ('truth'), not plural ('truths'); certain, not doubtful; absolute and unconditional, not relative; and grounded in God's infinite knowing, not in our tiny capacity to know anything. As Jean-Paul Sartre acknowledged, in words that faith is happy to reverse, 'There can be no eternal truth if there is no eternal and perfect consciousness to think it.'

With such a rock-like view of truth, the Christian faith is not true because it works; it works because it is true. It is not true because we experience it; we experience it, deeply and gloriously, because it is true. It is not simply 'true for us'; it is true for any who seek in order to find, because truth is true even if nobody believes it and falsehood is false even if everybody believes it. That is why truth does not yield to opinion, fashion, numbers, office, or sincerity; it is simply true, and that is the end of it. It is one of the Permanent Things. All that and a great deal more hang on the issue of truth, even though this is only the lesser argument for truth.

The final reality

The greater argument for the importance of a high view of truth is that for both Jews and Christians, truth matters infinitely and ultimately because it is a question of the trustworthiness of God himself. In contrast, for western secularists final reality is only matter, a product of time plus chance, and truth to them has a corresponding status on that level.

As Darwinism has underscored more and more openly, natural selection does not favour a predisposition toward truth. On the contrary, 'truth-directedness' is a handicap, and a lack of it, as mentioned earlier with the fireflies, is an evolutionary advantage. This bias against truth quickly becomes practical. How does one support, let alone explain, the importance of truth from the perspective of secularist thinking? If Darwinism is right, perhaps human truth-directedness is part of our alienation, and therefore the entire project of the university and human truth-seeking is futile.

Secularists who choose to continue giving truth its higher status (as, for example, traditional journalists in opposition to the 'personal reportage' of New Journalism) have bestowed that status, not discovered it. A similar problem holds for the eastern family of faiths, including Hinduism and Buddhism. For both of these religions, the final reality is the undifferentiated impersonal. 'Truth', accordingly, is part and parcel of the world of human ignorance, bondage, and illusion (*maya*) separated from that final reality, which we must transcend.

Nothing could be a greater contrast to the high status of truth in the biblical view. Final reality for Jews and Christians is neither matter nor the undifferentiated impersonal, but an infinite, personal God. Infinite and yet

personal, personal and yet infinite, God may be trusted
because he is the True One. He is true, he acts truly, and
he speaks truly – for Christians, most clearly and fully in
Jesus, his effective, spoken 'Word'. God's truthfulness is
therefore foundational for his trustworthiness. His cov-
enant rests on his character; his truth can be counted on.

Jews and Christians are therefore immune to Darwin's
'horrid doubt'. In the biblical view, we humans can think
freely and can passionately pursue the full range of human
enquiry, from coffee-bar discussions to the strivings of the
noblest art to the tireless search for the scientific secrets of
the universe and knowledge in all fields. And all the while
we know that our intellectual powers and our very
disposition as truth-seekers are underwritten by the truthfulness of the Creator of the universe. As Pope John Paul
II writes in his encyclical on truth, this is all possible
thanks to 'the splendour of truth which shines forth deep
within the human spirit'. Truth transcends us as humans;
as we follow it, it leads us on, back, and up to One who is
true.

'In the beginning was the Word', John's Gospel begins
– which means that in the end meaning itself has
meaning, guaranteed by God himself and now spoken
forth as an effective, liberating Word.

In other words, for both Jews and Christians, truth is
not finally a matter of philosophy but of theology.
Philosophical issues are critical and, at least for
philosophers, fascinating, but the theological issue is
primary. For all the fragile precariousness of our human
existence on our tiny earth in the vastness of space, we
may throw the whole weight of our existence on God,
including our truth-seeking desires, because he is wholly
true.

If might makes right

What of those people who do not hold to traditional or biblical assumptions of truth but who care about society and their place in it? The response here might appear harder, and even, in the view of some, impossible. But in fact there are two powerful arguments for the importance of a high view of truth, even for those who do not believe in it. The first of the two is negative in nature: *Without truth we are all vulnerable to manipulation.*

The promise of postmodernism at first sight is a brave new world of freedom. 'Truth is dead; knowledge is power,' the exuberant cheerleaders tell us. We must all therefore debunk the knowledge-claims confronting us and reach for the prize: freedom from the dominations constraining us. What could be simpler and more appealing?

There is only one snag. What happens when we succeed in cutting away truth-claims to expose the web of power-games, only to find we have less power than the players we face? If truth is dead, if right and wrong are neither, and if all that remains is the will to power, then the conclusion is simple: might makes right. Logic is only a power conspiracy. Victory goes to the strong, and the weak go to the wall.

We can take the result in an individualistic direction, as Herbert Spencer did; a collective direction, as Karl Marx did; or a broad evolutionary direction, as proponents of the 'selfish gene' propose. But the result is the same. When everything is reduced to the will-to-power, manipulation is the name of the game and victory goes to the strong and the ruthless. 'Law!' Cornelius Vanderbilt once snorted. 'What do I care about the law? H'aint I got the power?'

The power can be subtle, too. One biographer wrote of

John F. Kennedy's manipulation as a master of 'using candor in lieu of truth'.

People would walk away 'thinking they've been told the truth. But, in fact, they've really been told nothing of true importance. The small and candid moments set up the big lie.'

In Lenin's famous formulation, there is always power and always manipulation. The question is forever 'Who? Whom?' Duke University professor Stanley Fish makes no bones about the outcome from the postmodern perspective. In an article entitled 'There's no such thing as free speech and it's a good thing too', he answers several common objections: 'Some form of speech is always being restricted ... We have always and already slid down the slippery slope; someone is always going to be restricted next, and it is your job to make sure that that someone is not you.'

Those who embrace postmodern power-playing are as suicidal as Aesop's eagle that, at the moment of its death, recognizes its own feathers on the offending arrow's shaft. To warn us of such folly, Solzhenitsyn and Havel stand as lone sentinels. Face to face with the force of a totalitarian propaganda and repression far worse than anything in the West, they took their stand on truth and could not be moved.

Fortunately for us, the test is not likely to come on such a cosmic stage. But the same principle holds true at humbler levels: the difficulty may be a controlling boss, a highly manipulative professor, or an emotional tyrant of a family member. Without truth we are all vulnerable to manipulation.

Pablo Picasso is a cautionary example. A genius as an artist, he was often a monster in his relationships, especially with women, because of his controlling, devouring personality. 'When I die,' Picasso predicted years before the filming of *Titanic*, 'it will be a shipwreck, and as when a big ship sinks, many people all around will be sucked down with it.'

When Picasso died in 1973, at the age of ninety-one, his prediction came true. Three of those closest to him committed suicide (his second wife, an early mistress, and a grandson) and several others had psychiatric break-downs. 'He amazes me,' said his friend, sculptor Alberto Giacometti. 'He amazes me as a monster would, and I think he knows as well as we do that he's a monster.' Indeed, Picasso referred to himself as 'the Minotaur', the mythic Cretan monster that devoured maidens.

One mistress, Marie Thérèse, described how Picasso set about painting: 'He first raped the woman and then he worked.' Another told him, 'You've never loved anyone in your life. You don't even know how to love.' Picasso him-self was brutally blunt, 'Every time I change wives I should burn the last one. Then maybe I'd be rid of them. They wouldn't be around now to complicate my existence.'

Picasso's destructiveness was rooted in his childhood but was reinforced by his early acquaintance with Nietzsche through friends in Barcelona. 'Truth cannot exist ... truth does not exist,' he used to mutter. 'I am God, I am God.'

Significantly, only one of Picasso's wives and mistresses, Françoise Gilot, survived him with integrity intact. She was forty years younger but not naïve. 'Picasso', she later wrote in *My Life with Picasso*, 'was like a conqueror, marching through life, accumulating power, women, wealth, glory, but none of that was very satisfying any more.' He was like Nietzsche's loveless superman who must suppress all caring: 'Love is the danger of the loneliest one.'

How did Gilot survive, well aware that it was foolish to be sucked into his orbit and fatal to come under his domination? The only safeguard, she said, was truth. Every day she had to be 'Joan of Arc, wearing one's armour from day till night.'

Freedom for

The second, and positive, argument for the importance of truth pales at first in comparison with the negative, but it is no less important. It is that *without truth there is no genuine freedom and fulfilment.* Isaiah Berlin, the great Oxford philosopher, used to remind students repeatedly that although freedom has two parts, many young people never experience the highest freedom because they appreciate only the lower.

Freedom, Berlin stressed, is both negative and positive. Negative freedom, or 'freedom from', has an obvious appeal in the modern world. Teenagers, for example, are famous for acting as if all freedom is freedom from parents, from teachers, and from supervision. Many adults make the same mistake.

Modern America, for example, has all the appearance of a nation-sized demonstration of the adolescent error writ large. Decisively parting company with the wisdom of their founders, Americans have exchanged the 'moral republic' of its framers for the 'procedural republic' of today. While the American framers wisely avoided the foolish opposition between authority and freedom of the European Enlightenment through their emphasis on 'tempered freedom' and 'ordered liberty', the present generation has overthrown their vision altogether. Whereas the framers believed that liberty requires virtue, virtue requires faith, and faith requires liberty (which in turn requires virtue, and so on), modern Americans believe only in 'due process' and the clash of competing self-interests in the neutral public square.

Many Americans equate freedom with privacy; as St Jean de Crèvecoeur observed, 'Nobody disturbs them', or as Justice Brandeis said, they want 'the right to be let alone'. They confuse unfettered freedom of choice with freedom of conscience; as Cardinal Newman put it, 'Conscience has rights because it has duties.' They lower freedom of speech to freedom to offend. They stress rights without responsibilities. And they mistake the lower and easier freedom, 'freedom under the rule of law', with the higher and harder freedom, freedom born of virtue that inspires 'obedience to the unenforceable'.

Yet negative freedom is always limited and incomplete without positive freedom. 'Freedom from' requires the complement of 'freedom for'. That is why, long ago, the Roman poet Tacitus wrote, 'The more corrupt the state, the more laws.' That is what Benjamin Franklin meant when he wrote, 'Only a virtuous people are capable of freedom.' Or what historian Lord Acton taught in his magisterial writings on liberty: freedom is 'not the power of doing what we like but the right of being able to do what we ought'. Yet having thrown over authority for the sake of reason, and now reason for the sake of desire, contemporary Americans find that the limitation of negative freedom becomes obvious: those who set out to do what they like usually end up not liking what they've done.

D. H. Lawrence came to the conclusion that stopping at negative freedom was a central problem of Americans: freedom was always left in declarations, the rage for rights, and the undying restlessness to 'move on'. He wrote in his essay 'The spirit of place':

Men are free when they are obeying some deep, inward voice of religious belief. Obeying from within … not when they are escaping to some wild west. The most unfree souls go west and shout of freedom … The shout is a rattling of chains. Liberty in America has meant so far breaking away from all dominion. The true liberty will only begin when Americans discover the deepest whole self of man.'

No-one expressed this point more often and more clearly than G. K. Chesterton in *Orthodoxy*:

The moment you step into a world of facts, you step into a world of limits. You can free things from alien or accidental laws, but not from the laws of their own nature. You may, if you like, free a tiger from his bars; but do not free him from his stripes. Do not free a camel from the burden of his hump: you may be freeing him from being a camel.

In other words, we are never freer than when we become most ourselves, most human, most just, most excellent, and the like. Yet, if this is the case, freedom has a requirement: the true, the good, and the free have to be lined up together. To be ourselves, we need to know who we are. To be fully human, we need to know what humanness is. To aspire after virtue, justice, excellence, and beauty, we not only need to know the content of these ideals but we need to practise them. After all, as the Greeks pointed out, if abstract virtue were enough, we could be virtuous while asleep.

In short, today the crisis of truth, tomorrow the corruption of freedom. Truth without freedom is a manacle, but freedom without truth is a mirage. If freedom is not to be vacuous and stunted, it requires truth – lived truth. As Pope John Paul II declared flatly when he was still a Polish cardinal under the Soviet tyranny: 'There is no freedom without truth.'

Will such arguments prevail? Not just in private life but in the public square? To be sure, we need to make them boldly, with imagination and compassion as well as force. But their strength lies in their pragmatism. If truth is truth, it reaches out a strong hand to men and women caught by abusiveness of a thousand kinds. If truth is truth, it strikes a chord in hearts everywhere that are yearning for deeper freedom. Truth, in sum, is far more powerful than mere talk about truth. Human beings are truthseekers by nature, and truth persuades by the force of its own reality.

FIVE

TURNING THE TABLES

'Oh, hang the world!' The large, somewhat sullen undergraduate could take no more. He slammed his fist on the table and rudely broke into the professor's speech.

'Let's give it a bad name first and then hang it,' the professor went on, unruffled, not realizing the mood had changed. 'A puppy with hydrophobia would probably struggle for life while we killed it, but if we were kind we should kill it. So an omniscient god would put us out of our pain. He would strike us dead.'

'Why doesn't he strike us dead?' the student asked.

'He is dead himself,' said the philosopher; 'that is where he is really enviable.'

The eminent warden of the college continued, 'To anyone who thinks, the pleasures of life, trivial and soon tasteless, are bribes to bring us into a torture chamber.' He was in full flood now, a disciple of Schopenhauer, as pessimistic as the old German and cynical too, with all the jaded brilliance of an academic on a well-worn theme.

Holding his glass of port, he went on, 'We all see that for any thinking man mere extinction is the ... What are you doing? ... Are you mad? ... Put that thing down!'

Dr Emerson Eames, distinguished Professor of Philosophy and Warden of Brakespeare College, Cambridge, found himself looking down the cold, small, black barrel of a cocked revolver in the hands of one of his brightest students, Innocent Smith.

'I'll help you out of your hole, old man,' said Smith with rough tenderness. 'I'll put the puppy out of his pain.'

'Do you mean to kill me?' the professor cried, retreating to the window.

'It's not a thing I'd do for everyone,' Smith said with emotion. 'But you and I seemed to have got so intimate tonight, somehow. I know all your troubles now, and the only cure, old chap.'

'It'll soon be over, you know,' Smith continued. And as the warden made a run for the window and leapt out awkwardly on to the flying buttress below, he followed him like a benefactor with a deeply compassionate look, the revolver in his hand like a gift.

Both men were surprised to see the first streaks of dawn. Their time together had begun nearly twenty-four hours earlier at Dr Eames's morning lecture. After a packed day, it had resumed late at night in the warden's rooms. Dr Eames, it was known, was always in for his friends and favourite students at any hour of the night.

'I came to see you at this unearthly hour', Smith had said as they started their ruminations, 'because I am coming to the conclusion that existence is really too rotten. I know all the arguments of the thinkers who think otherwise, bishops and agnostics and those sort of people. And knowing you were the greatest living authority on the pessimistic thinkers – '

'All thinkers', Eames had said, 'are pessimistic thinkers.' And with a weary cynicism he had kept up this depressing conversation for several hours until something in Innocent Smith had snapped.

Now, with the dawn breaking and Eames's legs hanging over the buttress and the buttress hanging over the void below, the mood changed again.

'The puppy struggles,' Smith said with pity; 'the poor little puppy struggles. How fortunate it is that I am wiser and kinder than he.'

'Smith,' said the philosopher, 'I shall go mad!'

'And so look at things from the right angle,' Smith sighed. 'Ah, but madness is only a palliative at best, a drug. The only cure is an operation – an operation that is always successful. Death.'

As he spoke, the sun rose, turning the sky from pigeon grey to pink. Bells rang, birds sang, the roofs of the ancient town were lit with fire, and the sun rose farther with a glory too deep for the skies to hold. Suddenly the unhappy man on the last morning of his life could bear it no longer.

'Let me come off this place. I can't bear it.'

'I rather doubt it will bear you,' Smith said, referring to the delicate stonework, 'but before you break your neck, or I blow out your brains, I want the metaphysical point cleared up. Do I understand that you want to get back to life?'

'I'd give anything to get back,' replied the unhappy professor.

'Give anything!' cried Smith; 'then blast your impudence, give us a song!' Which the startled professor was prodded to do, a hymn of gratitude for existence. Satisfied, Smith fired two barrels over his head and let him climb to the ground.

'I must ask your indulgence,' Smith said brokenly when they were together again. 'I must ask you to realize that I have just had an escape from death.'

'*You* have had an escape from death?' the professor said with irritation.

'Oh, don't you understand, don't you understand?' Smith cried. 'I had to do it, Eames. I had to prove you wrong or die. When a man's young he nearly always has someone whom he thinks the top watermark of the mind of man ... Well, you were that to me ... Don't you see that I *had* to prove you didn't really mean it. Or else drown myself in the canal.'

Smith continued, 'The thing I saw shining in your eyes when you dangled from that buttress was enjoyment at life and not "the Will to Live". What you knew when you sat on that damned gargoyle was that the world, when all is said and done, is a wonderful and beautiful place; I know it, because I knew it at the same minute.'

Ready to hand himself in and face being sent down from Cambridge, Innocent Smith finished with one last meditation.

'I mean to keep the remaining shots for people in the shameful state you and I were in last night – I wish we could even plead drunkenness. I mean to keep those bullets for pessimists – pills for pale people. And in this way I want to make this world like a wonderful surprise – to float as idly as the thistledown and come as silently as the sunrise; not to be expected any more than the thunderbolt, not to be recalled any more than the dying breeze ... I am going to hold a pistol to the head of the Modern Man. But I shall not use it to kill him. Only to bring him to life.'

Shortened and slightly retold, this inimitable passage is from G. K. Chesterton's *Manalive*. Fabulous and fantastic,

Chesterton's writing itself floats 'as idly as the thistledown'. And like his jesting Innocent Smith, he too holds his pistol to the head of Modern Man – and also to the head of start-of-the-millennium Postmodern Man and Woman – not to kill them but to bring them to life. And the story, of course, is not simply a flight of Chesterton's imagination but the fruit of his own life.

In 1892 Gilbert Keith Chesterton was an eighteen-year-old student at the Slade School of Art in London. Far from the stiff-upper-lip primness of the caricature of Victorianism, the end-of-the-century world of art was swirling with decadence, cynicism, and pessimism. Chesterton himself was also drawn to the macabre and the occult. In other words, his world was remarkably similar to our postmodern one.

But however much such pessimism and cynicism were the rage and however drawn to it he felt, one thing held Chesterton back: what he described later as a 'thin thread of thanks', a sort of 'mystical minimum of gratitude'. Bursting with gratitude for the gift of life, he was waking up to wonder as he set out to search for a philosophy that would allow him to be realistic and yet 'enjoy enjoyment' too.

In the course of his search, Chesterton not only came to faith; he came to faith by becoming an arch-sceptic about scepticism, a radical disbeliever in the fashionable disbelief. He found the sceptics and cynics not sceptical and cynical enough. Far from stopping short of tough questioning, the faith Chesterton came to was the other side of such questioning – and all the stronger for having gone through it.

Relativizing the relativizers

Chesterton's journey in life and his story in *Manalive* highlight an effective response to sceptics and those who insist on a radical relativism that is impervious to traditional claims to truth. Curiously, his approach is exactly the opposite of what most people try to do.

Advocates of traditional views of truth often respond to relativists in the same way as English or American tourists travelling in France who speak their English more slowly and loudly. Similarly, proponents of traditional views commonly underscore the objectivity of truth in ever more earnest and laboured ways. And then, when they fail to carry their point, they mask their frustration by issuing dire warnings of the consequences of disagreeing with them. The result is mutual incomprehension and a stalemate.

Chesterton shows us another way – in fact, two other ways – from an honoured tradition in Christian witness that is too often neglected today. For when it comes to belief and unbelief, no argument in the world is unarguable. Every argument either has been or will be put forth by someone. But while all beliefs appear consistent to those who believe them, they always have one of two problems: they are either constricting or contradictory.

In the first case the beliefs are more consistent but are incomplete in the sense that they are too small for the fullness of life. Chesterton calls this the problem of the madman: 'The strongest and most unmistakable mark of madness is this combination between a logical completeness and a spiritual contraction.' And in the second case the beliefs are more comprehensive but are inconsistent – which in the worst cases makes them self-refuting, a problem Chesterton calls 'the suicide of thought'.

Then comes the strategy used so well by Chesterton and the best protagonists of faith. The wilder and more dogmatic an argument is, the more important it is to argue against it on its own grounds. As Chesterton says, the principle stands that 'either we must not argue with a man at all, or we must argue on his ground, not ours'.

In this chapter we will explore two ways to do this, as put forward by Peter Berger as the two best ways to counter radical relativism. The first effective strategy for countering relativism on its own grounds is negative: '*relativizing the relativizers*'. By this is meant applying to sceptics the scepticism they apply to others, thus pushing them out toward the negative consequences of their own beliefs. With a good cigar and a glass of port, Chesterton's professor has one attitude toward life and death in his comfortable college rooms but quite another when hanging grimly to the buttress while staring down the barrel of a gun. When turned on him, his philosophy of life is cold comfort.

As Berger points out, the strategy rests on two assumptions. The first is that relativism and scepticism entail a hidden double standard: the relativism is inconsistent and incomplete. All too often, relativists relativize others but not themselves. They relativize the past but not the present. They pour the acid of their relativism over all sorts of issues but jealously guard their own favourite ones. A recent study of classical education in the universities points to this attribute when it defines the present-day western academic as 'a well-fed, elite, institutionalized thinker ... who crafts ideas for his peers, with the assurance that the consequences of those solutions should not and will not necessarily apply to himself'.

The strategy's second assumption is that consistency and clarity are linked. The task of encountering relativism,

Berger writes, is to 'see the relativity business to its very end'. Press relativism to its consistent conclusion and the result is surprising. Far from paralysing thought, relativism is itself relativized, the debunker debunked, and what emerges is an almost pristine realization of the importance of truth.

Wasn't this the assumption behind the prophet Elijah's challenge to Israel in the ninth century BC? If Baal, and not Yahweh, was God, then follow Baal, he cried as he offered the prophets of Baal the first opportunity to verify their god. With the bulk of the people sitting uneasily on the fence between God and Baal, Elijah knew that pious calls to return to God would have fallen on divided hearts and deaf ears. He had to mount the challenge on their grounds.

For if Yahweh is God, then Baal is not, and the fastest way for the people to see it was to push them toward the false faith that was bound to be falsified by reality. The disproof came first and cleared the ground for the proof, for with the false falsified the true could be verified. 'The LORD – he is God! The LORD – he is God!' was the people's conclusion with heartfelt conviction.

The same logic runs down through the centuries. Jesus said, 'By their fruit you will know them' – not by their seed. If you had spoken to the prodigal son the day he left home, would he have listened? If you spoke to him the day he hit the pigsty, would he have needed to? 'See where it leads to,' St Augustine advised in dealing with falsehood. Follow it out to 'the absolute ruddy end', C. S. Lewis remarked with characteristic Englishness. Push them to 'the logic of their presuppositions', Francis Schaeffer used to say.

In doing this, we need to beware of tripping over trivial contradictions or inconsistencies that don't matter much to the inconsistent: for example, Richard Dawkins's 'Show me a cultural relativist at thirty thousand feet and I will show you a hypocrite. Aeroplanes built according to scientific principles work.'

Similar examples of inconsistencies abound. Marxist sociologists may be adept at spotting 'exploitation' in a kindergarten but have immigrant nannies and pay their teaching assistants poorly. Smart-aleck sixth-formers may insist that 'everything is relative', yet will be the first to object if teachers mark their papers without any standards, such as 'I didn't like your paper; it's Tuesday.' Radical relativists may deny there are 'objective facts' but are strangely insistent on circulating highly detailed CVs. Postmodernist lecturers may claim that authors are without privilege in determining how their texts are interpreted, but woe betide the reviewer who misinterprets their latest contribution to scholarship and human knowledge. And so on.

All these examples betray relatively trivial contradictions that are more suitable for humour than for persuasive debate. But what counts is when the relativism matters to the relativist, when it becomes a question of life and not simply logic. In such cases the strategy and the logic are the same. The relativists' problem is not their clash with us but their contradiction with reality and therefore the cost to themselves.

When I studied philosophy as an undergraduate in the 1960s, an Arctic chill was still hanging in the air that froze any serious appreciation of religion. The source was the philosophy of logical positivism and the 'verification principle' of A. J. Ayer. Only that which could be tested by the five senses could be verified as true, he said. Theology was therefore 'non-sense,' or, as it was famously said, 'The word G-O-D is less meaningful than the word d-o-g.'

The trouble for A. J. Ayer was that his verification principle couldn't verify itself: it was self-refuting. For to accept as truth only what can be tested by the senses is a principle that itself cannot be tested by the senses. It too is non-sense. Ayer's approach, he later admitted, was 'a blind alley'. Years later I enjoyed a conversation with him on the train between London and Oxford. Although retired and knighted as Professor Sir Alfred J. Ayer, he was candid about the failure of his principle. 'I wish I had been more consistent,' he said. 'Any iconoclast who brandishes a debunker's sword should be required to demonstrate it publicly on his own cherished beliefs.' Indeed.

Again and again the lesson is simple: while no argument is unarguable, *some thoughts can be thought but not lived.* So we should never stop halfway in dealing with scepticism, but follow ideas uncompromisingly to their conclusion. When heads collide with the wall they will have reached the limits of their position and will be open to reconsider. In this sense, reality is what we run into when we are wrong, for when we are right, we don't run into it. 'There are times', Václav Havel wrote, 'when we must sink to the bottom of our misery to understand truth, just as we must descend to the bottom of a well to see the stars in broad daylight.'

The crisis is the opportunity

The strategy of 'relativizing the relativizers' has both a sobering and encouraging side. The sobering side arises from the fact that ideas have consequences. The tactic can easily be reduced to a game – and a heartless one – but this obscures its real mercy: because the sceptics' view is finally untrue, it is in their interest to discover it in good time. But even if we care so little that we say and do nothing, life itself will most likely push the sceptics out to face reality anyway, and the final outcome may be far less pleasant.

Put differently, all people at some point behave true to their beliefs. Sooner or later they will act on the assumptions they truly hold and reap the consequences. We often say that people don't 'live up to their beliefs', but it would be more accurate to say that, in a crunch such as temptation, they switch to other beliefs and live up to those instead. We do live by our beliefs. The question is, which ones?

Now although someone's beliefs and assumptions may not be true and do not describe reality, they will still drive his or her behaviour. So if someone doesn't believe in truth, count on him to lie. If someone says there are no objective facts, expect her to be careless with facts to further her own interests. If someone explains everything by referring to evolution and the 'selfish gene', be sure that at some point he will be extremely selfish on behalf of the fitness of his own survival. If someone describes newborn babies as 'replaceable' and of no more value than snails, you can bet that she will become an advocate of 'involuntary euthanasia' (in other words, murder), and so on.

The principle also holds true for nations, for ideas have consequences. Differences make a difference. Behaviour follows beliefs as surely as thunder follows lightning. What starts in the studies will end in the streets. When it comes to postmodernism, the stunning fact is that we do not have to predict its consequences: we have already seen the influence of its core ideas on history. Do we really imagine there can be no consequences a second time around?

Not far from his death in 1951, French writer André Gide reflected on the influence of intellectuals on the moral and cultural weakness of France in the first half of the century. He dismissed the scapegoating of writers and the smearing of whole eras and schools. He emphatically rejected the Fascists' charge that the intellectuals had 'discouraged and devitalized' French youth. But still, he acknowledged that his generation of artists had come 'under Nietzsche's spell' and introduced a power-worshipping vitality and barbarism to France.

> Yes, Zarathustra bewitched too many of us with his dangerous catchwords. Let us be hard! Let us defy the code of Christian ethics! Re-evaluate all values! … How thrillingly adventurous life seemed, up there, in glacial height, immeasurably beyond all good and evil. How enthralling it was, to disregard all conventions, to transgress all taboos. The call of instinct and intuition; the worship of energy; the panegyrics of *élan vital* – it was stirring and in-toxicating. But from Nietzsche's Power philosophy it is only one stop to Sorel's *Defence of Violence* and to Spengler's *Decline of the Western World*.

'The decline of the Western world … *C'est la faute à Nietzsche* (It's Nietzsche's fault),' he concluded. But also, 'Why not admit it? I too have sinned and have contributed my bit to the general disarray.'

Will we live to see a similar *mea culpa* from the postmodern thinkers similarly bewitched by Zarathustra? From writers who have trashed the reality of words and lawyers who have ridden roughshod over the sanctity of law? Will we hear a genuine, unconditional apology from President Clinton acknowledging that, far from defending his Constitution, he drove a bulldozer through the rule of law and the delicate fabric of trust underlying the republic? We shouldn't hold our breath. But unless a significant number of his nation's thinkers and leaders see what has happened and rise to repair the breach, the consequences are only a matter of time. As Nietzsche said of his prediction, this tremendous event is still on its way.

Yet the strategy has an encouraging side too. The crisis, at its very worst, is the opportunity. The darkest night is just before dawn. In terms of distance, the prodigal's pigsty is the farthest point from home; in terms of time, the pigsty is the shortest distance to the father's house. That is one reason people of faith are not overcome by crises. As Chesterton wrote in *Orthodoxy*, 'If any frightened curate still says that it will be awful if the darkness of free thought should spread, we can only answer him in the high and powerful words of Mr. Belloc, "Do not, I beseech you, be troubled about the increase of forces already in dissolution. You have mistaken the hour of the night: It is already morning."'

Pointing out the signals of transcendence

Berger's first strategy for countering relativism, relativizing the relativizers, is unashamedly negative. This in itself leaves some people uncomfortable, and an added problem occurs when people use the approach in a purely logical way. In searching for any and all 'contradictions', they end up being tiresomely fussy and unconvincing.

In contrast, the real task is to be prophetic, not pedantic; to search for contradictions that matter – and matter not to us but to the people we are engaging. In other words, the goal is to look for the contradictions between logic and life, to search for the tension between the relativism or scepticism of their philosophy and the 'treasure of their heart'. Only the latter will become a smart bomb to detonate fresh thinking.

Because of the negative nature of the first strategy, many people are more drawn to the second tactic for countering relativism on its own grounds, which is entirely positive: *'pointing out the signals of transcendence'*. By this is meant the strategy of drawing attention to the contradiction and yearnings within people's beliefs that point beyond those beliefs towards entirely different possibilities.

Whereas 'relativizing the relativizers' is negative because it highlights the negative consequences of false assumptions, 'pointing out the signals of transcendence' is positive because it points toward the positive conclusions of true aspirations, unnoticed before. In the comfort of his room Dr Emerson Eames is mired in his Schopenhauerian gloom, but when confronting the starkness of death in the beauty of dawn, an enjoyment of life begins to shine in his eyes. This first contradicts his put-the-puppy-out-of-its-misery pessimism. Then instinctively, intuitively, irrepressibly, and undeniably, his gratitude to be alive punctures his pessimism and points beyond it to the possibility of higher meaning in life. Gratitude quite literally became Eames's pointer toward salvation, just as it did for his creator in real life.

Peter Berger defines signals of transcendence as 'phenomena that are to be found within the domain of our "natural" reality but that appear to point beyond that reality'. His discussion of them in *A Rumour of Angels* includes some signals that are positive (for example, order, humour, and hope) and some that are negative (for example, his 'argument from damnation').

The best-known example of a positive 'signal' in real life is C. S. Lewis's being 'surprised by joy' – having experiences that prodded him toward being a 'lapsed atheist' and set him off on a search for meaning. But Berger's argument from damnation is particularly powerful and common, as in the poet W. H. Auden's experience that stopped him in his tracks and turned him around to start his journey toward faith.

In 1939, Auden emigrated to the United States. In November, two months after the outbreak of the Second World War, he went to a cinema in the Yorkville district of Manhattan. The area was largely German-speaking, and the film he saw was a Nazi account of their conquest of Poland. When Poles appeared on the screen, he was startled to hear people in the audience shout, 'Kill them! Kill them!'

Auden was stunned. Amid all the changes of heart and mind he had passed through in his life, one thing had remained consistent: he believed in the essential goodness of humanity. Now suddenly, in a flash, he realized two things with the force of an epiphany. On the one hand, he knew beyond any argument that 'human nature was not and never could be good'; the reaction of the audience was 'a denial of every humanistic value'. On the other hand, he realized that if he was to say that such things were absolutely evil, he had to have some absolute standard by which he could judge them.

Here, Auden realized, was the fatal flaw of his liberalism: 'The whole trend of liberal thought has been to undermine faith in the absolute.' Or as he remarked to a friend, 'The English intellectuals who now cry to Heaven against the evil incarnated in Hitler have no Heaven to cry to.'

Spurred by this contradiction-cum-yearning, Auden left the cinema on a quest to renew his 'faith in the absolute' and began the journey that led him to faith in Christ.

Auden's realization throws light on one of the deepest problems of postmodernism: its inability to look evil squarely in the eye. In its levelling of moral standards and glorifying of power, postmodernism has close ties to the forces that gave rise to Nazism. But it would be unfair to lay the responsibility for the 'blond beast' at Nietzsche's door. For instance, it was his sister Elizabeth, rather than Nietzsche, who was virulently anti-Semitic. But an even deeper criticism of Nietzsche is undeniable. By insisting that nothing is good or evil in itself, or the 'same for all', Nietzsche shows that he had not faced the reality of evil squarely.

In 1947 Thomas Mann wrote *Nietzsche's Philosophy in the Light of Contemporary Events*, especially the revelations of Auschwitz and Treblinka. 'How bound in time, how theoretical too, how inexperienced does Nietzsche's romanticizing about wickedness appear ... today! We have learnt to know it in all its miserableness.' More than half a century on, one can only pray that America, as the dominant player in the West, does not become the second former-Protestant country to undergo that dark lesson.

Put differently, have you ever heard an atheist exclaim 'Goddammit!' *and mean it?* We can all be taught not to judge; we can all be told that there are no moral absolutes. But when we come face to face with raw, naked evil, then relativism, non-judgmentalism, and atheism count for nothing. Absolute evil calls for absolute judgment. Instinctively and intuitively, we cry out for the unconditional to condemn evil unconditionally. The atheist who lets fly 'Goddammit!' in the face of evil is right, not wrong. It is a signal of transcendence, a pointer toward a better possibility – and unwittingly a prayer.

A full discussion of these strategies would take us beyond our immediate purpose. But the central point is plain: neither strategy is purely theoretical; both are practical, powerful, and proven. Postmodern forms of relativism, scepticism, cynicism, and the like may appear to shatter traditional convictions to smithereens. But fears that such views are beyond argument are groundless.

For no human being lives outside the reality common to us all. Whatever people may say the world is or who they are, it is what it is and they are who they are. Again, no argument is unarguable, but there are thoughts that can be thought but not lived. When all is said and done, reality always has the last word. The truth will always out. Standing up to falsehood, lies, and crazy ideas is never an easy task, but (as we explore next) it is far easier than the hardest task of all, becoming people of truth ourselves.

SIX

ON RECORD
AGAINST OURSELVES

'I was a posthumous child. My father's eyes had closed upon the light of this world six months when mine opened on it …' This sentence, one of the first in Charles Dickens's *David Copperfield*, has struck a chord in many readers in a fatherless world. 'No memory, no emotion,' Albert Camus wrote of his father, who died in 1914 at the Battle of the Marne when he was only a few months old. Friedrich Nietzsche was a little older when his pastor father died, but the same sense of orphaned loss pervades his view of life, including the 'death of God'.

Dickens's words fascinated a small, twelve-year-old French boy, who later wrote, 'I tried to work things out on my own with this book and this sentence, which was really very intriguing.' Born in Paris on 6 February 1932, he felt he was not just an only child but an unwanted child. He had rarely been with his mother before he was three, and what love he experienced had come not from his parents but from his grandmother.

In fact, he had been born to an unmarried teenage mother and an unnamed father. And while his mother's parents had sent her off to another neighbourhood because of the shame of illegitimacy to a good Catholic family, his grandmother had at least stopped the illegal abortion his mother desired. And when his mother neglected him, his grandmother had taken him into her home. So he owed both his life and early love to her.

But when his grandmother died, the boy went back to his mother and her new husband, his newly adoptive father, and things grew rapidly worse. His parents were climbing enthusiasts whose membership in the French Alpine Club was virtually their religion. Looking back, he later told of how every spring when their holiday came round, the question would come up, '"What are we going to do with the kid?" The underlying thought, which they didn't even bother to hide from me, was always – "How can we get rid of him?"' Not surprisingly, excluded from their holidays and left behind when they celebrated Christmas in the mountains, he recollected, 'I know each time I was terribly depressed.'

When he was twelve, he stumbled on to his family secret. Rummaging in a cupboard when his parents were out, he discovered a small almanac belonging to his father. In it were all the family's special events – birthdays, journeys, celebrations – but nothing for 6 February, his birthday. Stunned, and with his suspicion now aroused, he searched further and several weeks later came upon the family record book. There he discovered that the woman who made him feel a 'nuisance' was indeed his mother, but his real father was, and remained, unknown. The 'father' whose warmth and humour he appreciated was not his father at all. From then on, whenever he laughed at the man's jokes he felt a pang of sadness.

From that point the family relationships spiralled down. With the parents drawing ever closer together and shutting out the unwanted son, and the son seeking ever wilder revenge, the outcome was predictable: truancy, alcohol, drugs, crime, solitary confinement in a juvenile detention centre, and two suicide attempts.

Little wonder that years later, when his most autobiographical (and first successful) film came out, film director François Truffaut, hero of the French New Wave in the 1950s and '60s, was torn in two by the response. On one side was the wild adulation of success at the Cannes Film Festival and with the wider film-going public, but on the other was the shock and anger of his estranged parents who resented their portrayal in *Les Quatre cents coups* ('The 400 Blows').

Truffaut kept his promise to his adoptive father. The day the film opened, he publicly denied that it was autobiographical: 'If the young Antoine Doinel sometimes resembles the turbulent adolescent I was, his parents bear absolutely no resemblance to mine, who were excellent …' But no-one was fooled. The truth was, as Truffaut had made clear in earlier interviews, that becoming a film director was his way of settling the score with his miserable childhood and delinquent adolescence. Life was his screen, the screen was his life, and his films revealed the scars of his painful road to freedom.

Explanation, not excuse

Unquestionably, childhood loomed too large in twentieth-century thought. Thanks to Sigmund Freud, its hang-ups and wounds were used to justify too much and to excuse the most outrageous flights of irresponsibility and victim-playing. But the opposite position is no better. We are right to judge things as true or false, right or wrong, prudent or foolish, beautiful or ugly, but when we refuse to notice the influence of personal factors we are exercising blindness. President Clinton, for instance, acknowledged that nineteen of the twenty characteristics of an adult child of an alcoholic apply to him.

In the same way, we can legitimately assess François Truffaut's films alongside those of Alfred Hitchcock, David Lean, Steven Spielberg, or whoever. But we miss much if we don't see them also as the products of Truffaut's journey in life.

Films, in fact, were integral to Truffaut's response to his clandestine childhood, as was his *auteur* (author) theory of film-directing. At first he had tried to win his parents' approval through model behaviour. When left at home as a boy, for example, he would repaint rooms and upgrade old electrical wiring. But when that failed, he engineered his escape from misery through the world of imagination, devouring three books a week and sneaking out to three movies a day. Reading, Truffaut said, was the best way of escaping a mother who 'could stand me only if I was silent' (a line he used later in *The Man Who Loved Women*).

Increasingly, Truffaut also resorted to lying. As one biographer wrote, 'François would also make up stories, lying compulsively as a way to settling his score with reality.' Covering for his truancy from school one day, he came up with the famous reply put in the mouth of his hero fifteen years later, 'It's my mother, sir ... She died.'

As time went on, the line between Truffaut's imagination and lying was worn away. His psychiatrist at the detention centre, whom he called the 'spychologist' in *Les Quatre cents coups*, described him as a youth 'using repeated lies to escape' his background. For instance, he developed a talent for reading newspaper accounts and describing the scene so closely that his friends thought he had been there. And one of his favourite early films was Sasha Guitry's *The Story of a Cheat*.

Truffaut's relationships were touched by lying too. Although ultimately he believed that couples could not last harmoniously, he always claimed to be seeking the 'ideal woman'. From eighteen on he developed the habit of concurrent relationships. Each of several women was simultaneously lovable and essential to him because different (as in *The Man Who Loved Women*). 'I write them worn-out lies,' Truffaut told a friend. 'They respond favourably to these letters which are all feverish declarations of love (success no doubt stems from the fact that I'm not sincere).'

Where can we draw the line between Truffaut's imagination and his lying? Between the wounds he received and those he inflicted? Between his prodigious talent and his prodigal self-indulgence? In 1973, when his friend and fellow-director Jean-Luc Godard came out of Truffaut's *Day for Night*, he attacked Truffaut angrily: 'Probably no-one else will call you a liar, but I will.' François was sleeping with his leading actress, Jacqueline Bisset, as he usually did when he made movies, but that wasn't the impression the film gave: 'One wonders why the director is the only one who isn't screwing around in *Day for Night*.'

In our own lives, where do we draw the line between our childhood history and our adult responsibility? Most people, especially those who know their own hearts well, would not presume to judge. God only knows. But one thing is clear: when we take into account all the 'static' and 'interference' caused by personal considerations in our lives, living in truth can be seen for the challenge it is.

Living in truth is anything but a cliché or facile slogan; rather it is a strenuous and demanding way of life. Both the objectivity of truth and the subjectivity of our response to it form a sharp moral challenge. Earlier we saw that truth grows urgent when the discussion moves beyond philosophy and theory to engage the issues of public life. Here we face the uncomfortable fact that truth grows more urgent still when it goes beyond philosophy and theory to address character, morality, and personal history – ours.

Truth or nothing

The question of the personal distortions we each bring to truth raises the central challenge of living free. Such is the personal dimension of all our thinking and such is the dynamism and ultimate undeniability of truth as reality that it always confronts us with two choices: *either we conform the truth to our desires or we conform our desires to the truth.* Kierkegaard was so committed to the responsibility of this choice that he was nicknamed 'Either/Or'. 'I who am called "Either/Or"', he once said, 'cannot be at the service of anybody with both/and.'

Stated baldly in this challenge, the Jewish and Christian view of truth flies directly in the face of modern views, just as we saw earlier with postmodern views. Expressed most powerfully in the Enlightenment, the modern view of truth made two claims: first, that truth is objective, certain, and knowable by the unaided intellect without the interference of personal distortions; and second, that the freer the thinker, the more he or she is committed to the fearless pursuit of truth at any cost. The biblical position rejects both these claims as pretentious and false. As human beings we are by nature truth-seekers; as fallen human beings we are also by nature truth-twisters. And a proper account of truth in the human project must do justice to both.

The Enlightenment view was expressed in the motto *Sapere aude* (Dare to know), set out in a famous essay by Immanuel Kant in 1784. It underlies all the purported contrasts between faith and reason, such as the age of faith being the 'Dark Ages' while the age of reason is the 'Enlightenment', and so on. As Bertrand Russell wrote typically, although in contradiction to the facts, 'Among philosophers, belief seems to me generally purchased by some sacrifice to truthfulness & so I find myself combating it.' The contemporary writer A. N. Wilson displays the same attitude, accusing Cardinal Newman of the 'sin against the intellect' simply because he held to Christian faith.

Unfortunately for protagonists of the Enlightenment, both these claims have been shown up as self-serving myths – and here the Christian ranges solidly on the side of postmodernism against modernism. To be sure, the ranks of the Enlightenment include thinkers for whom truth was a magnificent obsession. Years earlier in the *Republic*, Plato described philosophers as those with 'no taste for falsehood; that is, they are completely unwilling to admit what's false but hate it, while cherishing the truth'. Similarly, in his *Ethics* Aristotle wrote that the person who loves truth for the very sake of truth 'when nothing is at stake will be still the more truthful when someday everything is at stake'.

Max Weber was such a man. Arguably the greatest of all social scientists, Weber passionately pursued the ideal 'Truth or nothing' – similar to Emily Dickinson's 'My Country is Truth' and Albert Camus's 'Prefer truth to everything.' One day late in Weber's life, asked by a friend why he pressed on with his research despite the pessimism of his conclusions and his earlier breakdown, he replied fiercely in words that echo Nietzsche, 'I want to see how much I can stand.'

Few thinkers match Weber's courage and dedication to truth. But people of faith are among those who do: for instance, Rabbi Menahem Mendi (the 'Kotzker'), who had one word on his banner, *Emeth* (Truth); or Søren Kierkegaard, whose answer to the question 'What do I want?' in the last year of his life was, 'Quite simply: I want honesty.'

More importantly, as mention of the 'brooding Dane' reminds us, passion for truth is no guarantee of immunity from personal distortions in pursuing truth. The 'psychology of knowledge' should take its place alongside the sociology of knowledge. And this is where the story of the Enlightenment and its modernist thinkers turns out to be most surprising.

Paul Johnson's *Intellectuals* is a fascinating study of the great minds that helped make our modern world. Rousseau, Shelley, Marx, Ibsen, Tolstoy, Hemingway, Brecht, Bertrand Russell, Sartre, and others – Johnson examines the men and women of ideas who have risen to replace the guardians of traditional society and who on the basis of their unaided intellects now prescribe our remedies and direct our future.

Scrutinizing their record, both personal and public, Johnson focuses specially on their moral credentials to tell us how to conduct our lives. His evidence is startling and his conclusion sober:

> The belief seems to be spreading that intellectuals are no wiser as mentors, or worthier as exemplars, than the witch doctors or priests of old. I share that scepticism. A dozen people picked at random on

the street are at heart as likely to offer sensible views on moral and political matters as a cross-section of the intelligentsia. But I would go further. One of the principal lessons of our tragic [twentieth] century, which has seen so many millions of innocent lives sacrificed to improve the lot of humanity, is – beware intellectuals.

Such accounts of western intellectuals leave the myth of the dispassionate Enlightenment truth-seeker in tatters. The real situation is almost the opposite: the cleverer the mind, the slipperier the heart, or (expressed more carefully) the more sophisticated the education, the subtler the rationalization. Erudition lends conviction to self-deception. Anyone not convinced should read the thinkers themselves. One of the most brazen examples is Aldous Huxley, author of *Brave New World*.

In his earlier book, *Ends and Means*, Huxley admits that he 'took it for granted' that the world had no meaning. 'I had motives', he wrote, 'for not wanting the world to have meaning; consequently assumed that it had none, and was able without any difficulty to find satisfying reasons for this assumption.'

Huxley reached his view of the world, in other words, for 'non-intellectual reasons' and then rationalized it – that is, he provided reasons other than the real reasons. Unashamedly embracing a humanist bad faith, he digs his hole deeper: 'It is our will that decides how and upon what subjects we shall use our intelligence.' After all, he continues in his bizarre public confessional, 'The philosopher who finds no meaning in the world is not concerned exclusively with a problem in metaphysics. He is also concerned to prove that there is no valid reason why he personally should not do as he wants, or why his friends should not seize political power and govern in the way they find most advantageous to themselves.'

Anyone for a postmodern faith before its time? Any bidders for a secularist faith that flaunts itself as bad faith, a self-serving projection, a life-lie for the elite, and an ideology in the full-blown definition – a set of intellectual ideas that serves as a social weapon for his and his friends' interests? Huxley pleads guilty on every count, or rather, he brassily trumpets his position as a manifesto. 'For myself, no doubt, as for most of my contemporaries, the philosophy of meaninglessness was essentially an instrument of liberation.'

Needless to say, few writers are so revealing as Aldous Huxley. But he is not alone in his truth-twisting. Alfred C. Kinsey's groundbreaking *Sexual Behaviour in the Human Male* turns out to be based on flagrantly flawed and fraudulent data. Feminist revolutionary Betty Friedan, author of *The Feminine Mystique*, misrepresented herself shamelessly; far from being a stifled suburban housewife, as she depicts herself, she was a communist activist and propagandist with a full-time maid. Celebrated deconstructionist and Yale professor Paul de Man was discovered to be a former Nazi collaborator with an appalling record of lying and deception; writer Mary McCarthy described him as having 'an intelligence that's outdistanced his morals'. Along with an embarrassingly long list of western thinkers, they illustrate the first of the two choices offered us by truth: they attempt to conform truth to their desires rather than conforming their desires to the truth.

Nietzsche was candid about this first strategy. 'It is our preference that decides against Christianity, not arguments.' Criticizing the Stoics in his *Beyond Good and Evil*, he accuses them of pride in imposing their views on nature: 'You would like all existence to exist after your

own image – as an immense glorification and general-
ization of Stoicism.' But today, he says, this happens with
any philosophy: 'It always creates the world in its own
image.'

And what philosophers do, others do too. George
Bernard Shaw recognized what T. E. Lawrence was really
promoting in the myth of 'Lawrence of Arabia'. He was
out to sell something. More importantly, he was out to
find something – his identity. Shaw wrote to him, 'I note
that you have again moulded the world impossibly to your
desire. There is no end to your Protean tricks … What is
your game really?'

The element of bad faith in postmodernism is striking.
Many postmodern thinkers are refugees fleeing from the
collapse of Marxism. While hankering after its radical
critique of society, they are reluctant to face up to its
bankruptcy. David Horowitz, a former socialist radical
himself, argues that 'Leftism is a crypto-religion.' Indeed,
it is a bad faith in the classic sense of believers believing
because of fear of the alternative. But left-wingers refuse to
acknowledge the fact because 'to the Left, the alternative is
unthinkable. They are inside a community of faith and to
leave it would mean leaving every friend you had, and
joining the people you thought were evil. It would drain
your life of all its meaning. So the Left has deep blinders'
that stop it facing reality.

Truth's two options turn on more than a play on words.
Conforming the truth to our desires is easier in the short
term but harder in the long. The strategy allows us to
remain in control but it leads us away from reality and
therefore requires rationalization. Worse, because it takes
us away from what is real and true, it inevitably ends in
disappointment.

For instance, Huxley was later to abandon his early

position as unsatisfactory and head in the opposite direction, toward eastern mysticism.

Conversely, conforming our desires to the truth is harder in the short term but easier in the long. We give up our need for control and submit to truth outside us which, if we were wrong about truth before, requires repentance rather than rationalization. We have to face up to reality rather than trying to fit reality into our schemes. But the long-term outcome is freedom because, as we saw, truth is freedom and we are engaging with reality as it truly is.

The most radical relativism of all

An important piece of the puzzle still remains. Why is it that the Jewish and Christian view holds together two aspects of truth that the modern and postmodern views separate? For on the one hand the Jewish and Christian faiths join the modern thinker to insist on the objectivity of truth, while on the other they stand with the postmodern thinker to acknowledge the subjectivity we bring to truth, including our own personal distortions. Within the biblical view, humans are truth-twisters as well as truth-seekers.

The apostle Paul sets out the answer in his magisterial letter to the earliest Christians in the imperial capital, Rome. Describing the belief (or unbelief) of those to whom the good news of Jesus is coming, he says that they are 'holding the truth in unrighteousness'.

Sometimes translated as 'suppressing' or 'stifling' the truth, Paul's idea may be captured in the modern experience of hijacking. A plane is flying to its scheduled destination – say, from London to Geneva – but a hijacker can put a gun to the pilot's head and fly the plane to Algeria. In the same way, Paul argues, truth is truth with its own God-given reality and logic, but someone who refuses to believe in God is attempting to hijack truth and force it to fly to his own destination. In this sense, all human unbelief 'holds the truth in unrighteousness'. It seeks to conform the truth to its desires.

Put differently, unbelief in the biblical view is not passive, an innocent but inaccurate view of the world that has unfortunately 'got it wrong' at a few points. Rather, unbelief is active, driven by a dark dynamism. In fact, the Bible says, behind unbelief lies the most radical relativism of all: a relativity born not of culture, race, gender, class, or generation but of sin, the claim to the 'right to myself'. In Nietzsche's words, which here coincide with St Paul, as soon as any philosophy or belief begins to believe in itself, 'It always creates the world in its own image; it cannot do otherwise.' Philosophy is 'this tyrannical drive itself, the most spiritual will to power, to the "creation of the world"'.

Here is the root of the ultimate relativism and of the deepest distortions we each bring to reality. The central problem in knowing is not the world (or race, class, gender, and generation, as postmodernists believe), but the self. The autonomous self bows to no-one and seeks to be the sole arbiter of life and truth. The claim to the 'right to myself', which includes the claim to the 'right to my view of things', is the reason we do not naturally conform our desires to the truth but try to conform truth to our desires – and in the process 'hold truth hostage'. Our use of reason itself is not only wounded and weakened but made wilful and wrong by sin.

Unless this relativity is addressed and the standard of absolute truth brought back into the picture, our love can never escape being self-love. And our self-knowledge can never rise above self-deception. As the Greek statesman

Demosthenes said, 'Nothing is easier than self-deceit. For what each man wishes, that he also believes to be true.' What Nietzsche said of his former friend, Richard Wagner, will be true of us all: he does not believe in God, 'but he believes in himself. Nobody who believes only in himself can be entirely honest.' As T. S. Eliot wrote in his *Four Quartets*, 'Humankind cannot bear very much reality.'

Elsewhere in Paul's writings and throughout the Bible the full force of this radical view of human believing emerges. Disbelief has many faces. Sometimes it is an act of suppression, turning truth away from its natural ends. Sometimes it is an act of exploitation, turning truth toward our own ends. Sometimes it is an act of subversion, turning truth inside out and upside down; Paul writes that unbelievers worship the creature rather than the Creator and lies rather than truth. And sometimes it is an act of self-deception or delusion, because the claim to the right to myself and my view of things means turning a blind eye to all other ways of seeing things, especially God's.

But underneath all the denial, there is always tension in unbelief because the truth remains the truth even when we 'hold truth hostage'. Or as St John writes in the prologue to his Gospel of Jesus the Word, 'In him was life, and that life was the light of men. The light shines in the darkness, but the darkness has not understood it.'

No-one has done more to develop this theme than St Augustine. 'Falsehood', he wrote in *Confessions*, 'is nothing but the existence of something which has no being.' Or again, 'Man's love of truth is such that when he loves something which is not the truth, he pretends to himself that what he loves is the truth, and because he hates to be proved wrong, he will not allow himself to be convinced that he is deceiving himself. So he hates the real truth for the sake of what he takes to his heart in its place.'

The insistence on self-deception in human knowing is strong in Jewish and Christian thought. In Jewish mystical literature, the world of the here and now is called the 'world of falsehood'. The Kotzker's one goal in conversation was to say to people: 'Undeceive yourself!' Abraham Heschel writes, 'So many people become salesmen to their delusions ... A person living a lie and taking it to be the Truth moves in a world of self-delusion.' From a very different perspective, D. H. Lawrence argued the same:

> Man is a thought-adventurer. He has thought his way down the far ages ... which brings us to the real dilemma of man in his long adventure with consciousness. He is a liar. Man is a liar unto himself. And once he has told himself a lie, round and round he goes after that lie, as if it were a bit of phosphorous on his nose-end. The pillar of cloud and the pillar of fire wait for him to have done. They stand silently aside, waiting for him to rub the *ignis fatuus* off the end of his nose. But man, the longer he follows a lie, becomes all the surer he sees a light.

Descending downward

This radical diagnosis of the personal distortions in knowing has challenging consequences for living in truth. A generation ago philosopher Simone Weil warned her fellow-citizens in France, 'We live in an age so impregnated with lies that even the virtue of blood voluntarily sacrificed is insufficient to put us back on the path of truth.' Albert Camus spoke similarly of the difficulty of fighting a lie in the name of a half-truth already shrunk to a quarter-truth. As we sink back down to that world of murky grey once again, two antidotes are urgent: an accurate diagnosis of 'living the lie' and an effective remedy restoring us to 'living in truth'. Perhaps the simplest and most helpful diagnosis of the degeneration toward living-the-lie is philosopher J. Budziszewski's description of the 'seven degrees of descent' on the downward path of dishonesty.

The first step down is 'simply sin'. We lie because we have done wrong. Lying becomes the secondary utility sin in the service of some primary sin.

The second step down is 'self-protection'. As Budziszewski writes, 'Lies are weaklings; they need bodyguards.' Each new protective ring of lies breeds its own protective ring until the liar is smothered in layers of lies and lying.

The third step down is 'habituation'. Lies repeated become habits, and habits repeated become character. Before too long a single lie becomes a settled way of lying and we cross the border between lying and becoming a liar.

The fourth step down is 'self-deception'. The more we lie, the more we lose hold of truth and the more we succumb to believing our own lies. Sincerity and self-deception then reinforce each other.

The fifth step down is 'rationalization'. Believing our own lies, we give explanations other than the real reasons for all we do. Then we blame our weak grasp of truth on the weakness of truth itself, so that (for example) postmodernism itself becomes a gigantic rationalization for our contemporary lack of truthfulness.

The sixth step down is 'technique'. The more accomplished we are as liars, the more lying becomes our craft. Hitler's technique of the 'Big Lie' was simply the tactic that a big falsehood repeated over and over is more effective than a small one. Statistics – as in 'lies, damned lies, and statistics' – are an obvious modern equivalent.

The seventh and lowest stair is that 'morality turns upside down'. As Budziszewski observes, 'the moment lying is accepted instead of condemned, it has to be required. If it is just another way to win, then in refusing to lie for the cause or the company, you aren't doing your job.' Thus living-the-lie replaces living-in-truth, and, in the moral murkiness, truth and freedom are lost and evil is born.

Needless to say, this description illuminates but does not reverse the downward path. What is also required is the effective remedy, which for Christians is rooted in the strenuous discipline of 'living in the light'.

Practising truth

As we have seen, living in truth has consequences on many levels, but it all begins and ends with the personal – with each of us as we really are when we stand alone before God. As the apostle John wrote, in words that are magnificent but searching, 'God is light and in him there is no darkness at all. If we claim to be sharing in his life while we go on living in darkness, our words and our lives are a lie. But if we live in the light as he himself is in the light, then we share a common life, and the blood of Jesus his Son cleanses us from all sin.'

John's awe-inspiring vision of living in truth as 'living in the light' is the secret of the deepest integrity that seeks to overcome the personal distortions in our dealings with truth. On the one hand, we face the challenge of practising the truth. For truth does not offer itself as convenient and user-friendly; nor does it come to us from someone else's mind ready-made with 'no assembly required' — a sermon, a lecture, a seminar, or a tip transferred from one mind to another as if on a computer disk. Knowing always entails more than knowing will ever know, so the deepest knowing comes only in doing. The task of living the truth requires that we stake on it our very existence.

On the other hand, we face the challenge of practising the truth before God. To become true we must live bathed in the full floodlight of One who is true. Only when we realize that all our pretences, evasions, and fig leaves are useless can we achieve the honesty and humility needed for change. As Abraham Heschel used to say, going far beyond Socrates, 'An untransformed life is not worth living.'

Let me underscore what I said in the introduction. In writing about this vision I do not pretend always to be living up to it. But one thing is as fatal to this vision as hypocrisy: the piety that reduces it to a cliché. And this takes us back again to the challenge of the dilemma with which truth faces us squarely.

For those who seek to conform the truth to their desires, the key word is *compartmentalize*. This is the practice of cordoning off a part of life that may be unpleasant and insistent so that, by putting it into a separate compartment, we can go on living as if it wasn't there. The notion was made popular by President Clinton, who learned it from his mother as a coping mechanism. As the president's mother wrote in her autobiography, 'Whatever is in someone's past is past, and I don't need to know about it ... When bad things do happen, I brainwash myself to put them out of my mind.'

But the trouble is, compartmentalizing is a form of split-screen living. 'Brainwashing oneself' is another term for suppressing truth or 'holding the truth in un-righteousness'. Convenient in the short run, it is disastrous in the long run. It should be blamed roundly for the lack of integration it causes and named clearly as the lack of integrity that it is.

In contrast, for those who seek to conform their desires to the truth, the key word is *confess*. This is the act of acknowledging to someone else that we have done wrong. As such, it is an act of faith with three parts: an announcement of what we believe to be true and good; an acknowledgment of where we have fallen short; and an alignment to which we are committing ourselves. Confession therefore provides the mid-course correction that realigns us with truth as many times as we need to be.

To be sure, confession has often been abused as an instrument of institutional control: for example, by the Christian church or the communist party. And it is often distorted today by those who confuse it with the voyeurism of tabloid television or by the makeover artists of therapeutic engineering who manipulate it to their own ends.

But compartmentalism doesn't deserve the good name it has, whereas confession doesn't deserve its bad name. For, rightly understood, confession pivots on a stunning truth that is an act of great moral rarity: *in making a voluntary confession to someone else – God above all – we freely go on record against ourselves.* As G. K. Chesterton wrote in *What's Wrong with the World?*, 'When a man really tells the truth, the first truth he tells is that he himself is a liar.'

Hence the liberating and reordering force of confession and the priceless value of those whose close fellowship makes it possible for us to confess without shame. For instance, a friend of mine has a friend with whom he has built such intimate fellowship and accountability that he calls him his 'conscience partner'. St Augustine, writing from a monastery, uses the term 'true brothers' to describe such a relationship. In a famous passage in *Confessions*, he says, 'But my true brothers are those who rejoice for me in their hearts when they find good in me, and grieve for me when they find sin. They are my true brothers, because whether they see good in me or evil, they love me still.'

Whatever the term, what matters is the practice. For Christians, belief in the absolute power of truth means not holding the pretence of our own absolute truthfulness. We know that while we are still on earth we will never be perfectly true. Nor do we believe that truth-telling means 'complete authenticity' and 'total transparency'. These ideals are therapeutic, not Christian, and are impossible to attain and dangerous to attempt. Talk of authenticity and transparency quickly degenerates into pseudo-intimacy, coercive openness, and public undressing that are the emotional equivalent of communism and the recipe for the notoriety-therapy of tabloid television: 'Keep nothing to yourself'/'Demand to know everything about everyone else'/'The more humiliating the more healing' – at least for the peeping public.

Total trustworthiness is hard enough. There was good reason for the old saints' assertion that it is more appropriate for a sinner to pray than to vow. Not all promises will be kept, and we will never plumb the depth of our own self-deception. Yet under God, 'true brothers' and sisters are living mirrors to show us that truth is personal and moral as well as factual. And that our task together is to be demonstrators of truth and therefore worthy children of the God of truth.

None dare call it cliché

As I said in the introduction, this is a little book on a big topic and many doors have been left unopened. But I trust that our exploration has established at least three things: first, the gravity of the present crisis of the truth in the western world; second, the wisdom of lifting the debate out of its rut as a controversy between the 'modern' and the 'postmodern' views; and third, the richness and strength of the positive biblical vision of living in truth. God laughs at those who think they have killed off truth, yet reaches out to all who long for its rock-like safety.

For people of faith whose book is the Bible, truth can never be mere theory, let alone one that is sterile and contentious. Truth is the direct representation of reality – that which throbs with created life, and that which is given and guaranteed by the Creator who is himself the final reality. God is truth just as God is love. He speaks truly and he acts truly.

Because love of truth is love of God, wilful error is unfaithfulness and apostasy is adultery. He requires truth in all who approach him, not just in words and deeds but in their innermost hearts. They – we – must not just debate the truth, we must know the truth. If we would live free, we must not just know the truth, we must live in truth and we must become people of truth. As Kierkegaard wrote in *Training in Christianity*: 'The truth consists not of knowing the truth but in being the truth.'

That is the sort of truth that 'prevails'. That is the sort of truth whose one word 'outweighs the entire world'. That is the sort of truth that 'sets free'. Yet that is also the reason that, while truth is freeing, it is far from free: truth asks of us everything in our lives that contradicts it. It is impossible to experience love without being truthful and it is impossible to discover truth without loving it. As Kierkegaard wrote in his journal, 'You cannot have the truth in such a way that you catch it, but only in such a way that it catches you.'

A century and a half ago, Alexis de Tocqueville underscored the political requirement for living free. 'If a man has no faith he must obey, and if he is free he must believe.'

Over fifteen hundred years ago, St Augustine expressed in his prayer to God the personal requirement for living free. 'You have made us for yourself and our hearts are restless until they find their rest in you.'

Two thousand years ago, Jesus of Nazareth said to his followers words that declare his universal requirement for living free – words that are sober fact for children as well as the old and all in between; for the poor and powerless no less than the beautiful, the rich, and the important; for people of both genders, all races, every class, and each generation: 'If you stand by my teaching,' Jesus said, as the Word, the Logos, the very meaning of meaning speaking into the world, 'you are truly my disciples; you will know the truth, and the truth will set you free.'

The dawn of the third millennium finds the western world in a quandary over one of its most vital foundations – truth. Caught between a tarnished modernism and a dangerous postmodernism, between a view of truth (part arrogant and part naïve) that is no longer credible and a view of 'truth' (part sceptical and part gullible) that every day grows less desirable, the West is at odds with itself, its past, and its future.

At such a moment the view of truth that originally inspired the West shines clearer than ever. Anchored in the very meaning of the universe, capable of simple application as well as sophisticated analysis, a spiritual and moral requirement with vast implications for the whole of life, the biblical (Jewish and Christian) view of truth has the strengths of the modern and postmodern views, the weakness of neither, and just one snag: the cost of its unsparing moral challenge.

Which brings us back to where we began. The West (and its lead society) are at a crossroads. In a world of lies, hype, and spin, there is an urgent need for people of truth at all levels of society. There is quite simply no other way to live free. The choice is ours. So also will be the consequences.

FOR FURTHER READING

William J. Bennett, *The Death of Outrage: Bill Clinton and the Assault on American Ideals* (Free Press, 1998)

Peter L. Berger, *A Rumour of Angels* (Doubleday, 1969)

Dietrich Bonhoeffer, *The Cost of Discipleship* (SCM Press, 1964)

G. K. Chesterton, *Orthodoxy* (Hodder and Stoughton, 1996)

Jacques Ellul, *Propaganda* (Alfred A. Knopf, 1965)

Os Guinness, *The Call: Finding and Fulfilling the Central Purpose of Your Life* (Word, 1998)

Václav Havel, *Living in Truth* (Faber and Faber, 1989)

Abraham Joshua Heschel, *A Passion for Truth* (Farrar, Straus and Giroux, 1986)

Roger Lundin, *The Culture of Interpretation* (Eerdmans, 1993)

Alasdair MacIntyre, *After Virtue: A Study in Moral Theory* (Gerald Duckworth, 1981)

Aleksandr Solzhenitsyn, *The Oak and the Calf* (Harper and Row, 1979)

Dallas Willard, *The Divine Conspiracy* (HarperCollins, 1998)

GRATEFUL ACKNOWLEDGMENTS

As a writer who writes only from time to time and always in the gaps and around the edges of a busy life, I am more aware than most writers of the large debt of gratitude I always owe. In this case of this book:

To Bud Smith, the Chairman, and the Trustees of the Trinity Forum, whose friendship, commitment, and support in pursuing our overarching vision are an inspiration and encouragement.

To Dick Ohman, Karen Erickson, Ginger Koloszyc, Duffy Lott, and Gordon MacDonald, my Trinity Forum colleagues whose dedication, hard work, and fun make collegiality a daily pleasure.

To Debi Siler, whose help in typing the manuscript was unfailingly fast, cheerful, precise, and a real tonic.

To Parks and Micheline Shipley, for the generous loan of their home on the Chesapeake Bay, which acted like a burst of acceleration to the writing.

To Amy Pye, my US editor, and Paul Engle, my US publisher, whose skill and wisdom transform an arduous task into a near-pleasure.

To Mike Cromartie, Bill Edgar, and Dick Ohman, whose reading and critique of the first draft of the book saved me from many errors and was invaluable to the final version.

And to David Aikman, Mark Berner, Mike Cromartie, Bill Edgar, Doug Holladay, Bob Kramer, Skip Ryan, Bud Smith, Ralph Veerman, David Wells, and Michael Woodruff, who have been my Augustine-style 'true brothers' and great friends over many, many years.